Dog *friendly*
Pub Walks

Seddon Neudorfer

Wet Nose
Publishing Ltd

www.countrysidedogwalks.co.uk

First published in 2014. Reprinted in 2015 and February 2017

by **Wet Nose Publishing Ltd**,

All enquiries regarding sales telephone: 01824 704398
email cdw@wetnosepublishing.co.uk
www.countrysidedogwalks.co.uk
ISBN 978-0-9573722-7-6

"Who are you calling 'half pint'?"

Contents

Introduction

The twenty walks included in this book are all designed so that you and your wet nosed friend have a really enjoyable time. Where there are stiles, they are specially designed with lift gates for dogs. However, both the Elterwater and the Scout Scar walks have stone steps to pass over stone walls. At a quick glance there is information at the beginning of each walk to tell you what to expect and what you may need to take with you. The descriptive guides will also warn of any roads ahead or areas of livestock so that you can get your dog on the lead well in advance.

Dogs just love to explore new places. They really enjoy the new smells and carry themselves a little higher with the added excitement. Going to new places gets you and your dog out and about, meeting new people and their dogs. It is important to socialise dogs, as they will be more likely to act in a friendly manner towards other dogs as they gain confidence.

The stunning pictures in this book are just a taster of what you can see along the way. Many of the walks have fantastic views and scenery. Some of the walks are wooded, offering shade on those hot summer days.

The walks are graded Easy, Medium and Challenging. They are all around one to three hours long, depending on your and your dog's pace. You may start with the easy ones and work up to the challenging walks depending on your and your dog's fitness. Different dog breeds and dog age must be taken into account when you decide which walks to do.

Different breeds of dog have different levels of fitness. For example, bulldogs can only do short walks whereas a border collie or a springer spaniel are extremely energetic and difficult to tire out. It is recommended that you do some research on the breed of dog that you own to get to know what sort of exercise that they require.

You may have a walk that you are happy doing with your dog every day, but this book will show you new areas to explore with a change of scenery and a chance to meet new people and their dogs. Dogs love new places to visit and you will see the change in them as they explore the new surroundings, taking in the new smells with delight. You will fulfil both your life and your dog's just by trying somewhere new.

Some of the walks include bridleways, so you may encounter horses and cyclists. It is important to put your dog on a lead if you see horses approach. It is always helpful to say hello to the riders as they near so that the horse realises that you are not a threat.

The Lake District National Park

The Lake District Naional Park was formed in 1951 to protect the beauty of the mountainous landscape and tranquil lakes from being developed into housing and industry. Most of the National Park is owned privately. Roughly 25% belongs to the National Trust and only 3.9% belongs to the Lake District National Park Authority. The villages and farmland only add to the beauty which complement the natural landscape, with its heathlands, hedgerows and beautifully crafted stone walls that are blanketed in moss and the quaint cottages and beautiful houses that have been built from local stone.

Ground Nesting Birds

Watch out for vulnerable ground nesting birds during 1st of March until the end of July. Dogs that stray off the main paths may disturb birds and chicks, possibly killing them or breaking eggs. Species to look out for are Sky larks, Meadow pipits, Curlew, Red and Black grouse, Snipe and Pheasants.

Some if not all of these birds are declining in numbers, due partly to their vulnerability when nesting. Dogs are a threat to them, even if treading on them unintentionally. Some other threats are foxes, badgers, stoats, weasels, birds of prey and crows. Please help to protect these birds during the nesting season by keeping your dog on the paths when walking in open areas such as grassland, moors, heathland and scrub.

Rivers

Some dogs love water and will think nothing of plunging into the river. With the extreme weather conditions over the last few years, a river that may be safe for your dog to swim in can change in a matter of hours to become a swollen torrent that could wash your dog away. Please be careful when near rivers if there have been heavy periods of rain or if they look swollen or fast flowing. It is best to put your dogs on the lead, until you have assessed the situation.

Dogs and Alcohol

Please note: alcohol is poisonous to dogs!

Throughout this book there are jokes about dogs drinking alcohol, this is intended as humour by humanising dogs in funny situations. Any dog pictured drinking beer is only supping alcohol-free drinks and it must be stressed that dogs should never be given alcohol.

Pub Etiquette

All the pubs featured in this book welcome you and your dog, so you can relax part way around or at the end of a good walk. Dogs must be kept on a lead whilst inside the pub and we would ask that you consider other people. For instance, please don't allow your dog to lie down in the doorways or in thoroughfares. In wet weather, avoid your dog shaking his coat where he may spray mud onto people, which is not very pleasant, especially if they are eating. Remember, not all people like dogs, and some people may be allergic to them, or even frightened of them. If you consider this before going in it will help towards ensuring that the pub that you are visiting stays dog-friendly.

Livestock

If you find that you need to cross a field with cattle or horses and they seem interested in you or your dog it is recommended within the Countryside Code to let your dog off the lead. Never try to get between livestock and your dog. Your dog will get out of a situation a lot more easily with speed than you can. It is usually only cattle with young calves that are a threat, or young heifers or bullocks that tend to get a little inquisitive. They will usually stop when they get close to you or your dog.

Most horses will come over for a fuss but a small proportion do have a problem with dogs. They may see them as a threat and will act to defend the herd. Horses that are out with a rider are completely different as they are not defending the herd, and as long as you keep a safe distance there should not be a problem.

Sheep are not a danger to you, but your dog can be a danger to them. Where sheep are grazing it is vital that you have your dog on a lead or under very close control. You will know your dog, but if you are unsure it is better to play safe and keep your dog on a lead. It is important always to have your dog on a lead when around lambs. Lambs have a higher pitched bleat and can be the size of a cat, and your dog may act differently amongst them.

Ticks

If you have been walking in areas where sheep graze you should check your dog for ticks. They must be removed as soon as possible. It is best to use tick tweezers, which are specially designed to remove the head and leg parts of the tick. Ticks can carry diseases and the longer they remain latched on to your dog the more the chance of spreading infections.

Forests

The forest walks in this book are a changing landscape, which makes them unique and interesting. Descriptions may change with time, for instance a path may be described as being in the shade of the forest, but as this is a worked forest a section could be clear felled at any time. Another change over the years could be where a view is described across a previously felled area. This could then be planted up and trees grown blocking the views. Paths may change but this is less likely. On rare occasions the Forestry Commission may temporarily close paths due to forest works but again this is even less likely on a weekend. Any changes to the path networks that may occur after the date of print will be updated on our website.

Does your dog fetch a stick?

Most dogs love sticks and will pick them up without any encouragement from their owners. Vets and dog trainers recommend that you should not throw sticks for dogs. They can cause nasty injuries, sometimes fatal as the stick can pierce the throat, or rebound off the ground and cause harm to your dog.

Please clean up after your dog

Always be prepared, having dog bags with you at all times. Once you have cleaned up after your dog, please keep the bag, until you see a bin. If there are no bins provided, then take it away with you to a roadside bin. Dog bags that are discarded on the paths or in the bushes are unpleasant and unsightly and will not degrade.

1. **Wythop Woods** - The Pheasant

Nestling at the bottom of Sale Fell and close to Bassenthwaite Lake lies the tranquil and peaceful Pheasant Inn. Dating back to the 17th century this former haunt of the famous huntsman John Peel has been entertaining guests for the past 300 years in the traditional Cumbrian manner with stunning food and refreshment and good old fashioned values.

The hotel bar is the most famous and well known bar in the Lake District – it is full of local character! The décor and furnishings are unique and are a mix and match of days gone bye. Intimate, cosy, unique, and atmospheric are just some of the adjectives that spring to mind to describe the wonderful bar at The Pheasant! It's the perfect place to pop in during your walk. If you would like to stay for the night, dogs are welcome in the Garden Lodge Rooms.

Call: 017687 76234
www.the-pheasant.co.uk (check website for opening hours)

"Where's your owner?"
"Tied up outside."
"Same here."

Wythop Woods - Medium - 4.3 miles - 2hrs 30min

This medium walk has some ascents, but they are only for sections of the walk, and therefore the highest point is achieved without noticing any real climbs. A lot of the walk is forest, with some mixed woodland. On Sale Fell there are fabulous views across Bassenthwaite Lake and to the surrounding fells, with Keswick in the valley. The walk crosses farmland, where sheep may be grazing. There are a couple of quiet roads. There is a stream on route, where your dog can find water.

How to get there - From Keswick join the A66, signed for Cockermouth. After some distance, the road changes to a dual carriageway. Immediately as the dual carriageway ends, take the slip road on the left, which is signposted for The Pheasant Inn. Continue where you will see a small layby on your left. There are further laybys on your right, about 100 yards before reaching the Pheasant.

Grid Reference - NY 201307

Post Code - CA13 9YE

Parking - Free in Lay-by

You will need - Dog leads, dog bags

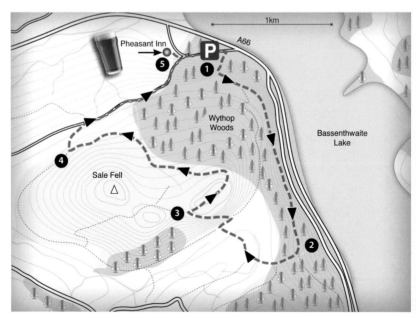

The Walk

❶ If you have parked in the first small layby, take the footpath on your left at the end of the layby. If you have parked in the larger layby, head back towards the busy main road, keeping your dog on a lead. Pass the private canoe/fishing car park on your left and continue on the road. Take the footpath on your right, just before another layby on your right, close to the main road.

Ascend slightly into the mixed broadleaved woodland. There are lots of ferns covering the ground. As you continue, coniferous trees dominate. Keep your dog under close control as shortly after you will meet a quiet tarmac road. Cross the road and continue on the footpath on the opposite side. You will pass a Forestry Commission yard on your far left. A short, steep rise brings you to another path and a tarmac road on your left. Ascend onto the road, listening out for forest vehicles.

As you climb you will gain views of Bassenthwaite Lake on your left. Keep your dog under close control as there is a busy road below on your left and there are no boundary fences. Ignore a forest track on your right. The track descends, where after leaf fall you will have views across the lake. Ascend again for about a quarter of a mile on this track. You will be rewarded with stunning views on your left of the lake and the surrounding fells. You pass some exposed rock on your right, and then your dog will find water on your right as it collects before going under the path. A turning bay for forest vehicles provides a wonderful viewing area on your left, and then just afterwards take the path on your right.

❷ Continue to ascend on the well-defined path as it twists and turns through the forest, passing exposed rock in places. On reaching a farm gate, put

your dog on a lead or under close control and pass through the gate. Continue straight ahead, keeping to the edge of the field, with a gorse bank on your right. Pass through another gate into another field. There is a stock fence on your right and mature hawthorn, which are the remnants of an old hedgerow. Ignore the farm gate on your right and continue through the farm gate straight ahead. Again, continue on the edge of the field, with a stock fence on your right. Pass a large pond on your right, beyond a stone wall. Pass an isolated farmhouse on your right, ahead. Ignore the path, which goes to the farmhouse and continue on the footpath. Pass through another gateway, keeping the remnants of a stone wall on your right. The remnants of the old hedgerow are at first on your right and then on your left.

Pass through another farm gate and turn right on the footpath. There is a hillside dominated by gorse on your left and farmland on your right. Look for a minor path on your left shortly after (about 100 yards). The path has a switchback as it ascends between the gorse. As you gain height, bracken and grasses replace the gorse. The views on your left and behind you are wonderful. Ignore the minor paths on your left and right. ❸ On reaching another grassy path, turn right and as you ascend there are views in all directions, with sea views on your left. As you reach a bench on your right, you will have amazing views over the lake to the fells beyond, with Keswick in the valley. You have reached the highest point of your walk: stop on the bench and enjoy a well-earned rest.

Continue on the worn path with one last short ascent, and then you begin to descend. Stay on the wider, grassy path, which descends to a stone wall. The path bends to the left, with the stone wall on your right, at the edge of a forest. The path soon veers away from the stone wall, descending between bracken. Cross a stream and on reaching a stone wall pass through a gate and continue straight ahead, descending on a grassy path with stunning views ahead. As you continue the path cuts across the hillside. There are views ahead and to your right.

Pass through a gap in the stone wall, crossing over old foundations of the wall, and continuing on the path with a chapel ahead. ❹ On reaching another path, turn right, putting your dog on a lead, and descend to the road, passing through a kissing gate. Turn right and descend on the quiet road, keeping to the right hand side, facing the oncoming traffic. Pass an old water trough on your right and Sale Fell House on your left. Continue through the village, ignoring a footpath on your right. Pass an entrance into the forest on your right and continue to descend on the quiet road. ❺ On reaching a road junction turn right, where you will reach The Pheasant Inn, where you can enjoy a well-earned pub lunch. When you leave the Pheasant turn right on the road. On reaching a road junction, turn right and continue on the road, where you will soon reach your car.

2. Barrow / Newlands Beck - Coledale Inn

The Coledale Inn is a genuine country inn situated above Braithwaite Village in a peaceful hillside position well away from passing traffic. It is ideally situated for either the walk along Newlands Beck or the more demanding walk around Barrow.

Walkers, families and pets are indeed given a warm welcome here. With twenty newly refurbished dog friendly rooms. All the rooms are en-suite and located in both the Georgian and Victorian parts of the hotel. They have TV and tea/coffee making facilities. The inn is extremely interesting in itself. It was built c.1824, starting life as a woollen mill, then a pencil mill, eventually becoming the licensed premises it is today. It is full of attractive Victorian prints, furnishings and antiques. From the moment you enter the welcoming Victorian residents' hallway, you will feel at home and comfortable at The Coledale Inn.

Tel: 017687 78272
Email: info@coledale-inn.co.uk (check website for opening hours)

"Last night we did the 'Sit, stay,...down'
- tonight it's....'down in one'..."

Barrow - Challenging - 4.2 miles - 3hrs
Newlands Beck - Easy - 3.5 miles - 1hr 30min

Both walks pass the foot of Barrow with stunning scenery, surrounded by fells. The Newlands Beck walk veers to the left to pass across farmland and then follows to the edge of the river, with farmland on your left. There is a stock fence allowing you to let your dog off the lead, providing the river hasn't become a torrent after heavy rainfall. The Barrow walk ascends on a footpath, at the foot of Barrow and Causey Pike. After some distance the path switches back ascending towards Barrow. You then come to a level, between Barrow and Outerside. The path then descends between the two fells to return to the village. There are sheep grazing throughout the Barrow walk and for some parts of the Newlands Beck walk.

How to get there - From Keswick follow the signs for Cockermouth on the A66. Turn left, following signs for Lorton and Braithwaite on the B5292. Continue on this road, passing through the village. On reaching the other side of the village, turn left following the sign for Coledale and Youth Centre, crossing a small road bridge. Keep to the road, which bends to the left (not the track straight ahead). You will see the Coledale Inn a little further along, on your left.

Grid Reference - NY 230234 **Post Code** - CA12 5TN

Parking - Free in the Coledale Inn car park.

You will need - Dog leads, dog bags

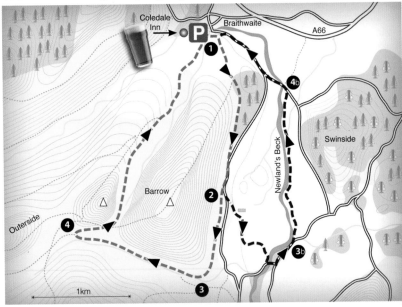

Dog Friendly Pub Walks - Lake District

The Walks

❶ Keep your dog on a lead to begin this walk. From the car park, go back out onto the road and turn right. Almost immediately turn left, following the finger post. Descend beside a driveway and pass a house on your left. Ignore a footpath on your right and continue straight ahead, between houses. Pass beside a river on your left. On reaching a road take the second right turn, passing a village shop on your right, following the sign for Newlands.

You will soon see a sign for Braithwaite Lodge and a bridleway on your right. Take this path ascending on the access road, between the stock fences. You are surrounded by hills in all directions, amongst the stunning scenery. Keep your dog on a lead, pass the farmhouse and stone barn on your left and go through the farm gate, between the two stone barns. Go through another farm gate straight ahead and ascend on the stone path. On reaching a stone wall, pass through a gate and turn left. Continue on the well-worn path, with stunning views on your left. Ignore a grassy path on your right and continue straight ahead, at the foot of Barrow, which is on your right, and woods on your left. Bracken dominates the hillside.

As you turn a bend you will have stunning views ahead of the fells, which have formed interesting shapes. After passing the woods on your left the views open up to the wider countryside across the Newlands Valley. The path descends, passing between gorse to reach a quiet road. Turn right on the road, where gorse lines your way, giving off the lovely coconut scent in the summer months. Continue on the road for some distance, passing a lay-by on your right. You will reach a sign for Uzzicar B&B. This is where the walk splits in two. If you want to continue on the Barrow walk continue reading the next paragraph. If you choose the easier walk then skip to the Newlands Beck heading.

Barrow - Challenging

❷ Continue on the road, until you reach a footpath on your right. Ascend on the stone path between the bracken. Pass some exposed stone on your right and as you climb, bracken is replaced by heather. There is a mountain stream visible below on your left.

❸ Ignore a path on your left and continue to ascend, where you will be surrounded by fells. Stay on the stone path, ignoring a grassy path, which veers to the left and ahead. Continue ascending for quite some distance. Below you will see small waterfalls as the river drops sharply in places. You will pass a very minor path on your right, which you may not notice. As you continue you will pass two minor paths, close together, where the stone path becomes separated with a rut in between. Continue ascending on the main path, where a little further on, just as you lose sight of the river, you will see an obvious path on your right, that cuts back on itself and starts off level, cutting across the hillside.

❹ Take this path, which will give you a break from your ascent as it cuts across the hillside, and then ascends gradually. You will have great views along the path that you have ascended on and back into the valley. The path bends to your left, and you will pass paths on your left and right. This spot is known as Barrow Door. The views here are exhilarating. You can see across Braithwaite into the valley and over to Bassenthwaite Lake on your left. On a clear day it is worth stopping for a while to enjoy it, resisting the temptation to steam ahead to the pub!

Now descend between the two fells, taking care if you need to keep your dog on a lead as the gravel and grassy paths can get slippery in wet weather. As you leave the gravel path, continue on the worn, grassy path, following close to the bracken on your right. Ignore a path on your right and continue straight ahead, now passing between the bracken. The path will reach a wider gravel path, where you continue to descend. Pass through a kissing gate and join a quiet tarmac road. You will continue to descend, passing several houses on your left. Ignore a footpath on your right and continue on the road, where you will reach the Coledale Inn on your left a little further along.

Newlands Beck - Easy

❷ Keep your dog on a lead and turn onto the access track for the Uzzicar Bed and Breakfast. Descend towards the farmhouse. Pass the driveway/ entrance to the farmhouse and continue on the track, which veers to your left, passing the chicken fencing on your left. Continue on the track, where you will reach a farm gate. Pass through the farm gate, keeping your dog under close control or on a lead and walk beside the stock fence on your left on the edge of the field.

At the end of the stock fence continue straight ahead, crossing the middle of the field. Turn left on reaching an old stone post, where you will see a waymarker. Follow beside the stock fence on your right, again to the edge of the field. The forested hill that you can see on your left is Swinside and fells surround you in the distance. There is a stream on your right as you continue between the fields.

On reaching the corner of a field pass through the gate and continue with the stock fence on your right at the edge of the field, beside the stream. As the stock fence turns a corner continue straight ahead, where you will reach Newlands Beck. Turn right and continue following upstream of the beck with a stock fence on your left. Put your dog on a lead and pass through the farm gate straight ahead, turning left on the road. Cross the road bridge and continue on this road, following signs for Portinscale and Grange. Pass a football pitch on your left and continue, close to the beck on your left.

❸b Take the next footpath on your left, passing through the gate, following signs for Braithwaite. Inspect the flow of the beck before letting your dog off the lead, as after heavy rainfall it can be fast flowing. Follow this well-made path for quite some distance. You will pass through a gate straight ahead and shortly after pass a lovely stone packhorse bridge. Continue on the path, where you will see Catbells on your right as you continue. You will have views to fells in all directions in the distance. As you reach close to a stone bridge ahead put your dog on a lead and continue to the gate. **❹b** Pass through the gate and turn left onto the quiet road, crossing the Little Braithwaite Bridge, which was re-built after the floods of 2009. Continue on the road for a short distance.

Turn right following the sign for Braithwaite, then as you reach the gable end of a farm building turn left and then right to pass the farm building on your right. Go through the gate and descend to the farm track, keeping your dog on a lead or under close control. Turn left and continue to follow the beck with farmland on your left. Pass through a farm gate straight ahead and continue following beside the beck. The beck will turn sharply to your right, where you now continue to cross a footbridge over another river. Turn left and follow on the edge of the field, beside the river.

Put your dog on a lead and pass through a gate into a caravan park. Stay on the footpath to the edge of the park, following the river on your left. Trees line the river here offering you a little shelter on hot days. Continue on the well-made path after leaving the caravan park and pass the houses to reach a road. Turn left on the road and then on reaching the road junction ahead turn left, crossing the road bridge and then turn immediately right. Follow beside the stream on your right, where you are now on a familiar path. Continue on the quiet lane and retrace you steps. Take the footpath straight ahead, where you will see the Coledale Inn straight ahead. You can now have a rest and enjoy a good pub lunch.

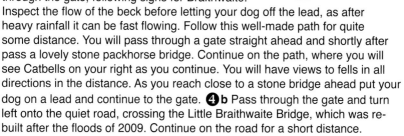

3. Swinside - Swinside Inn

The Swinside Inn is a traditional Lake District Inn and Bed & Breakfast, offering great food, dog friendly accommodation and panoramic views of the entire Newlands Valley and it's encompassing peaks. Located in the heart of the English Lake District, within an enchanting hamlet which sits in the entrance to the Newlands Valley, makes The Swinside Inn the perfect base for a walk with your dog.

This 300 plus year old Inn always has a very warm cosy welcoming atmosphere whatever the weather, in winter with it's two open log fires make it especially snug. In summer the south facing beer garden enjoys sun all day until the sunsets over the hills. The Refuge is a bar that has a wide selection of real ales, lagers, spirits & liqueurs..this fun themed bar is also a great place to relax after walking with your dog.

Tel: 017687 78253 l
www.theswinsideinn.com (check website for opening hours)

"Alcohol won't solve any of my problems...
but neither will biscuits and gravy!"

20

Swinside - Medium - 5 miles - 2hrs 30min

There is stunning hillside scenery all the way on this walk, and some fantastic shapes formed on the hill tops which surround you as you stroll in this beautiful valley. You will cross farmland, where sheep may be grazing, with beautiful mature trees, bracken hillsides, clear streams to refresh your dog and quiet hedge-lined roads. This is a valley that must be explored to fully appreciate its beauty. A stop half way at the Swinside Inn is the perfect place to get refreshed, before continuing your walk.

How to get there - From Keswick, take the A66 signed for Cockermouth. Turn left following the signs for Grange, Portinscale and Newlands Valley. Continue on this road, following for Grange and Newlands Valley. Continue following the sign for Newlands Valley. You will pass the Swinside Inn on your right. Continue on this road; turn left when you see the sign for Little Town. The sat nav will bring you to the edge of the village. Continue on a little further, passing through the village, where you will reach the car park, just before going over a little road bridge.

Grid Reference - NY 231193 **Nearest Postcode** - CA12 5TU

Parking - Car Park with charge at Little Town

You will need - Dog leads, dog bags

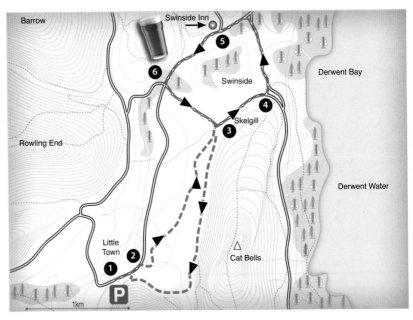

The Walk

1 From the car park head back towards the village, ascending on the quiet road, with a river on your left. On reaching the village, ignore a bridleway on your right and continue, passing Littletown Farm House on your left. Continue on the road, where a little further along you will see a public footpath on your right, signed for Skelgill.

2 Take this path, between the stone walls. At the end of the stone wall, pass through the gate on your left (not into the field), and continue along the track with a fence on your left and a bank on your right. Cross the footbridge at the ford and continue along the track, now with the river on your left and below. There are small gaps in the fencing, so if you have a little dog keep him under close control or on a lead as he may be able to get into the fields, where sheep are grazing. You will be surrounded by beautiful scenery, with sculpted hilltops in all directions as you continue through the valley. On reaching the end of the stone wall on your right, put your dog on a lead because sheep may be grazing and pass through the gate into a field. Continue along the track, which leads to another gate just before a house. There is a stream, where your dog may get a drink just before you pass through the gate.

After passing through the gate, continue on the well-worn track, cross a small stream (which may dry up during the summer months), and pass through another gate, beside the stile. You now continue across the middle of a field on a well-worn path. There are mature parkland trees as you continue amongst the stunning scenery. The path will become lined with well-spaced hawthorn, ash and oak, which are remnants of an old boundary hedgerow.

You will pass an old gate-post on your left and there are several small streams that cross over your path. After passing through a kissing gate, the remains of the old hedgerow continue on your left. At the end of the old hedgerow you will pass the end of a stone wall on your right. Continue straight ahead, crossing the field and heading for the stone wall in front of you. There is a gully on your right and another old hedgerow.

On reaching the stone wall pass through a gate and follow the fence line on your right. Pass through a gate into Skelgill Farm. The hills in the distance are known as the Skiddaw massif. Continue straight ahead on the obvious path. Pass through another gate, where you will pass amongst mature ash, sycamore and mixed pine trees. On reaching another gate, pass through it and continue between the farmhouse and the farm building, where you will go through another gate.

❸ Turn right onto a quiet access road, where you will see a lovely water trough on your right. Ascend the road and pass through a gate. You will now descend on the quiet road. If you look on your left in the distance you will see Bassenthwaite Lake. Continue on this road, passing a small car park on your right. ❹ On reaching the road junction turn left and continue to descend, following the signs for Portinscale and Keswick.

To avoid the cattle grid use the gate on your right. Continue to follow the road, which is lined with hedgerows and trees. You will pass a road on your right, signed for Hawse End Centre. Continue straight ahead, passing the Swinside Lodge on your left. The road then begins to ascend. Take the next road on your left, signed for Stair, Newlands Valley and Buttermere, and shortly afterwards turn left at the road junction.

Now ascend for a short distance with forest on your right and a copse of mature trees on your left. After passing the trees on your left you will gain wonderful views once more. ❺ You will soon reach the Swinside Inn, where you can have a good pub lunch.

Once refreshed, make your way back onto the road and turn right. Follow the road sign for Stair and Buttermere. Pass the houses and descend on the quiet road, where you can enjoy the wonderful scenery once more. Ignore a footpath on the right and continue on the road, passing another footpath on your right, where you will meet with a river on your right beside the road.

Dog Friendly Pub Walks - Lake District

6 You will pass a football pitch on your right and then take the first left turn, following the sign for Low Skelgill Farm and Catbells Camping Barn. Follow the quiet tarmac road, with farmland on each side of the stock fence and a hedgerow on your left. Continue to the end of the road, passing between the farmhouse and the barn. This section of the walk will be familiar to you. Ignore the footpath on your right. Ascend to the gate, pass through it, and then turn right after a few paces, following the sign on the finger post for Yewthwaite on the public bridleway. There may be sheep grazing.

Ascend on the gravel path with more beautiful hills ahead of you in the distance. The path cuts into the hillside, with a steeper section on your left. The area here is dominated with bracken. Stay on this path for quite some distance, surrounded by truly amazing hills. The hills ahead fan out into the distance. Ignore several paths to your left and right. The path follows a stone wall, which is replaced with stock fencing in parts.

The path can become a little rough in places, with large stones and some ruts. You will meet a quarried area. Just before the quarry, you will meet a fork; take the path on the left, which will skirt around the quarry, following the blue way marker. Pass the lower section of the quarry on your right. Turn right, before the higher section of the quarry, crossing a footbridge over a stream, where your dog can have a cool down.

Continue straight ahead on the obvious worn path, following beside a stone wall on your right. Ignore a path on your left and continue on the path, which descends toward the village. Pass some houses on your far right. The path then switches back to descend into the village. On reaching the familiar road turn left and descend, to retrace your steps back to the car park.

4. **Threlkeld** - Horse and Farrier (1688)

The Horse & Farrier has enjoyed an idyllic location in the centre of the picturesque village of Threlkeld, just 4 miles east of Keswick in Cumbria, for over 300 years. Built in 1688 and situated beneath Blencathra, with stunning views looking over towards the Helvellyn Range, this traditional Lakeland Inn offers a warm Cumbrian welcome to all its customers. Mellow Lakeland stone, traditional architecture and such a peaceful setting make the Horse & Farrier a perfect place to enjoy a quiet drink and delicious food after your walk.

The Restaurant is well known locally for the quality and imagination of its food and the Bar serves some of the best Jennings real ale in the Lake District. Dog friendly accomodation is also available for your dog walking holiday. The sister inn over the road, the Salutation Inn, also has dog friendly rooms available.

Tel: 017687 79688
www.horseandfarrier.com (check website for opening hours)

"A pint a day helps me work, rest and spray"

Threlkeld - Medium - 3.5 miles - 2hrs

This circular walk passes beside a lovely stream and then follows a river for quite some distance. You will have wonderful views over beautiful countryside to the distant fells. There are sections of open farmland, with grazing sheep.

Along the river there is a stock fence for most of the way, which prevents your dog from chasing the sheep. You will cross over a busy road at two points of the walk. The walk has a little section of ascent, but it is only gradual.

How to get there - From Keswick join the A66 following signs for Penrith. Take the turn-off which is signed for Threlkeld. Continue to the village and after passing a road on your right, take the next left hand turn onto Blease Road. Continue ascending to the edge of the village, where you will see the car park on your right. If you are following a sat-nav it will take you past the car park.

Grid Reference - NY 318256

Nearest Postcode - CA12 4SD

Parking - Free in the village car park

You will need - Dog leads, dog bags

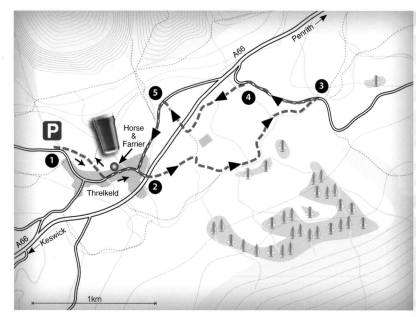

Dog Friendly Pub Walks - Lake District

The Walk

1 From the car park look towards the gable end of the house and take the footpath on your left, passing through a gate. Keep your dog under close control or on a lead, as sheep graze the field on your left. Descend to the river. Cross a footbridge and continue on the well-worn path, with the river on your right. Mature sycamore and oak line the river on both sides. Pass through another gate and continue on the path, now between fences so your dog can enjoy the water. However, keep him under close control as the village is a little ahead and there are gardens off the path. Continue following the river, cross another footbridge and proceed on the path.

Pass a picnic area on your left and ignore another footbridge. Put your dog on a lead and continue on the path, passing a house on your right and then a house on your left. On reaching the road turn left, you will reach the Horse and Farrier pub on your left. You can choose to call in now or on the way back. Continue on the road, passing the pub on your left. Take the next road on your right, just before reaching The Sally pub. Just before reaching the end of the road take the footpath on your right, keeping your dog on a lead. Follow beside the green chain-link fencing on your left. Pass through a gate and turn left on the pavement beside the busy dual carriageway.

2 Cross the busy road, just before reaching a left turn, using the middle island and then turn left. Turn right into a car park and pass Threlkeld Sports Pavilion on your right. Continue on the grassy path between the stock

fences, with farmland on either side, surrounded by fells in the distance. Pass through a kissing gate, keeping your dog under close control or on a lead as there may be sheep grazing. Cross the field on a slightly raised path, with stunning scenic views in all directions. On reaching the end of the field pass through the farm gate and turn right on the access road. Follow this road, turning left just before crossing the bridge. Check the flow of the river before letting your dog pass through the gate. The river may be swollen after heavy rainfall, so keep your dog on a lead or under close control if you think he may go in the water.

Pass through the gate and follow the footpath beside the river for some distance. Continue with the beautiful views on your far left and farmland beyond the fence on the left. The river current slows further along, as you turn a sharp left bend. Cross a footbridge, keeping your dog under close control, as there is only a wire fence on your left where small, determined dogs may enter. Cross a stream over the stone slab. Ignore several stiles on your left and continue. After another bend pass through a gate, turning left on the access road.

❸ Pass through a farm gate straight ahead, (not the one on your right) keeping your dog under close control or on a lead as there may be sheep grazing. Continue along the edge of a field on the access track, beside a stock fence on your right. Pass through another farm gate and continue, now ascending towards the farmhouse. Pass the farmhouse on your left and continue on the access track.

❹ On reaching a bend on the track, turn off the track to your left, crossing the footbridge and then follow beside the stone wall on your left at the field edge. Where the stone wall ends continue straight ahead and cross the stream via stones. Keep the row of mature trees on your left and continue to cross the field. The path veers to your right where it meets with the boundary hedge. Continue on the field edge, near to the main road, passing more mature scattered trees on your left. Shortly before reaching the edge of the field veer to the left, where you will see a waymarker and gate in the corner of the field.

Pass through the gate and turn right, putting your dog on a lead, as there is a busy main road ahead. On reaching the road, cross over with care and pass through a farm gate onto another access track, between the stock fences. At the end of the track turn left onto a wider access road. ❺ Pass through a pedestrian gate, beside the farm gate, and continue descending on the road. This road will descend into the village. On reaching another road turn right. Continue on this road, passing The Sally pub on your left, and then The Horse and Farrier on your right, where you can enjoy a well-earned rest before doing the last short leg of your journey. On leaving the pub turn right onto the road and take the next footpath on your right and retrace your steps back to the car park.

5. **Scales** - White Horse Inn

The White Horse Inn is a quintessential Country Pub with great pub food, open fires, local ales and a warm welcome. Located just outside the picturesque village of Threlkeld at the foot of the Blencathra and Sharp Edge, it is ideal for the finish of this walk with your dog. The owner, manager and staff are all dog lovers, so you and your dog are always welcome here. There is a dog friendly bunkhouse with four of the stables converted into bedrooms, two of which sleeping 6 people in bunks, one sleeping eight and one sleeping four.

The pub which is open from 11am to 11pm and has free wifi, hot drinks and good beer. Food is served 12-2pm and 6-9pm on weekdays and all day on weekends.

Tel: 017687 79883
www.thewhitehorse-blencathra.co.uk (check website for opening hours)

"Some blind date this is turned out to be. I'm getting the drinks in again and he's never off the 'dog & bone'..."

Scales - Challenging - 5 miles - 3hrs

This is an amazing walk, where you are rewarded with stunning views once you have ascended high enough. You will be walking amongst the fells of Scale, Blencathra and White Horse Bent, although not high enough to reach the peaks, so there are no sudden drops to worry about. You will be able to soak up the tranquillity of being surrounded by fells. There may be sheep throughout this walk. Streams pass under the paths, where your dog can get water. The descent can get a little steep in places, so care should be taken if you need to keep your dog on a lead.

How to get there - From Keswick, take the A66 signed for Penrith. Scales is signposted on your left, just after passing Threlkeld. You will reach the White Horse Inn immediately, as it is parallel with the A66.

Grid Reference - NY 343269

Postcode - CA12 4SY

Parking - Free in the pub car park

You will need - Dog leads, dog bags

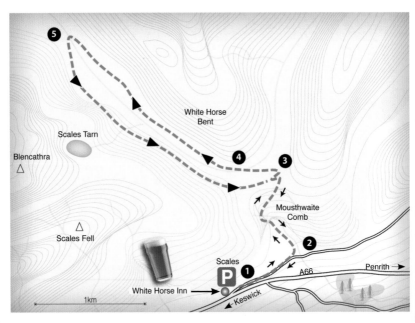

The Walk

1 Standing facing the pub, turn right and ascend on the quiet road, passing the overflow car park on your right. Keep your dog under close control or on a lead and listen out for traffic. Just before you reach a sharp bend, where the road descends, take the footpath on your left. **2** Dogs will need to be under close control or on a lead, as there may be sheep grazing. Pass through a gate and continue on the well-defined path. Juncus, a plant that thrives on boggy ground, dominates the grassland here.

The path ascends, gradually to begin with, for quite some distance. You will be able to make out your route ahead, where you can see the path as it cuts along the hillside, ascending to the horizon. As you ascend look behind you for beautiful views and take a break to get your breath back. Streams cross your path as you ascend, where your dog can get a drink.

As you near the top of the horizon you will cross over some exposed stone. If you go to the right it is a little easier, as the rock can be slippery in winter. After passing the rock, look back and take in the wonderful views across the landscape, surrounded by fells and mountains. The worn, grassy path now veers to your left, where you can see the fells in all directions. Look out for a minor path on your right, after about 30 yards. This path cuts back in the opposite direction. Stay on this path for a short distance, where you will reach a dip. **3** Turn left here, before the path goes up the hill.

Follow the worn, grassy path descending into the valley, between two fells.

A river flows at the bottom, and on reaching it, cross the footbridge. ❹ Here you can see the crystal clear water as it flows over the boulders.

Continue straight ahead, ignoring the more definite path on your right. Turn left a few paces on and ascend once again. The path joins a wider path, where you continue on your ascent in the same direction. The fell on your left is Scale Fell, where you can see your return path, cutting across the slope. The fell on your right is White Horse Bent. The ridge ahead is Sharp Edge, which is part of Blencathra. The path levels off for some distance and you will pass sections of scree. The path then ascends again, as you make your way to the dip on the horizon. As you near the top you will pass an eroded section of the path, crossing over scree. You will see the path again to the left of some exposed rock.

❺ On reaching the grassy path again, very close to the horizon, take the path on your left, heading back in the direction you came, but on the other side. Continue on this path, looking back down into the valley and across to the path which you have already taken. The path descends a little and you will then cross a stream, where you pass another section of scree, and then some exposed rock on your right. The path is now mostly level, with some undulating sections as it cuts across the hillside. The path veers to the right, where you cross another mountain stream, via the stones. Continue on the path, which is well-made here, having fixed flat stones as steps to descend easily.

The path then levels out again and views open up ahead as you continue. Ignore a path on your right and continue on the level path. You will eventually reach the top, where you will have panoramic views once again. Continue on the worn path, and where the paths split ahead, take the path on your right. The path bends to your right, where you are now on a familiar path. Cross over or around the exposed rock, with caution, especially if you have your dog on a lead. The path descends now, quite steeply, with loose stone. If your dog pulls on the lead, take care to ensure he doesn't pull you over. You will reach a familiar gate, and then the quiet road. Turn right on the road and descend to the White Horse Inn, where you can have a well-earned pub meal.

6. River Eamont - The Beehive

This pub is ideally situated for those who plan on entering the Lake District from Penrith. Why not stop here and walk your dog. At the end of a long walk, The Beehive is just what you need. This family run pub is all full of dog lovers, so you can be sure that you and your dog will always be welcome.

Inside it is bright, clean and tastefully decorated, with modern upolstery and polished wooden floor. An ideal place to relax, and in winter there is always a glowing fire to warm you.

Serving good homemade food from locally sourced produce. With a large play area outside and a friendly atmosphere, your whole family is welcome!

Tel: 01768 862081

"Yep, no probs...I can woof that down."

River Eamont - Easy - 3.2 miles - 1hr 30min

Starting at the Beehive Inn, this walk crosses the bridge to reach the river. You will follow this pleasant river, as it meanders through the quiet countryside, for a lot of the walk. If you are lucky you may see kingfishers and dippers along the way. You will reach Brougham Castle ruin as you leave the river. This walk does have some stiles. There are lift gates for for your dog, however they are inaccessible for very large breeds of dog. There are sheep grazing for parts of this walk and a quiet lane on your return, which brings you to Brougham Hall.

There is a very small section of busy road, with a pavement at the beginning and end of the walk.

How to get there - From Penrith, take the A6 towards Shap. Shortly after passing over the Eamont Bridge you will reach the Beehive on your left.

Grid Reference - NY 523284

Postcode - CA10 2BX

Parking - Free in the pub car park

You will need - Dog leads, dog bags

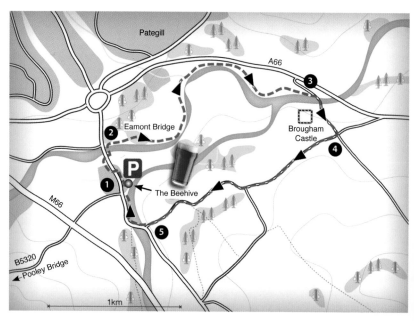

The Walk

❶ From the car park turn right and follow the main road, crossing over to make use of the pavement. Cross back to the other side before reaching the road bridge. Continue to the road bridge crossing on the pedestrian section. **❷** After crossing the bridge turn right and follow the footpath to Brougham on an access track, alongside the river. At the end of the track cross a stile on your left, using the lift gate for dogs. Cross another stile and then follow the footpath. After about 20 yards turn right. Continue on the footpath between the boundary fence of a house and a woodland copse.

At the end of the woods put your dog on a lead or under close control, cross a stile and continue on the edge of a field beside the river. This river may be fast flowing, so care should be taken to keep your dog out of the water. There are ducks along the river, which may tempt your dog in. You may also see kingfishers and dippers flying across the water. There may be sheep grazing.

Cross a footbridge beside a weir (the water current will be strong at the weir, so keep your dog on a lead here) and continue to follow the worn path beside the river. The path will come close to a busy road on your left for a short distance. Cross another stile and continue beside the river. You will reach a stock fence, which is the boundary to a private garden. Leave the river here, following beside the stock fence. After passing the house on your far right head for the kissing gate, veering to your left a little.

❸ Put your dog on a lead and pass through the kissing gate, where you will join an old tarmac road. Ignore a left turn which passes under the busy main road, and pass through the vehicle barrier. On reaching the road ahead turn right. Pass some houses and continue on the road, where you will have views of Brougham Castle ruin to your right. Continue on this quiet road.

❹ On reaching the end of the road, turn right and continue on this quiet country lane. You will pass a road on your left and continue straight ahead, following the sign for Pooley Bridge. Pass a house on your right, 'Rose Cottage'. After the bend in the road, pass several houses on your left. Continue, where you will pass a fort-like building on your left, known as Brougham Hall. Pass under a footbridge and continue on the road, descending, where you will reach a busy main road.

❺ Turn right on this busy road and continue. You will soon reach The Beehive Inn, where you can enjoy good food and a well-earned rest.

7. Surprise View - Mary Mount

Mary Mount is owned and run by the Mawdsley family, a hotel which offers a peaceful country house atmosphere. Set in idyllic surroundings on the shore of Derwent Water in the English Lake District, it is the ideal place to escape life's pressures. So part way through your walk go and enjoy the peace and tranquillity of this dog friendly hotel. The hotel is only yards from the Lodore landing stage of Keswick Launch on Derwentwater which maintains a regular service to Keswick and around the lake.

With its oak panelled bar and cosy lounge allocated for dog owners there is no better place for getting that complete rest during your walk. If you fancy staying for a few nights, there are dog friendly rooms available. All rooms are en-suite and as you'd expect, have TV and tea/coffee making facilities.

Tel: 017687 77223
www.marymounthotel.co.uk (check website for opening hours)

"oooh...I think I've had enough to drink!"

Surprise View - Medium - 3.2 miles - 2hrs

This is a stunning walk, with fantastic views over Derwent Water to Bassenthwaite Lake and the surrounding fells. The woodlands are delightful, being dominated by oaks in most parts, with moss-covered boulders and crags. You will pass many streams where your dog can get plenty of drinks and cool down. Views of Lodore Falls can be enjoyed and then the walk stops for a well-earned rest at The Mary Mount Hotel, where you can enjoy a good pub lunch, before continuing through woodland and then towards the end of the walk you can enjoy Derwent Water where your dog can have a dip. There is a stile with a lift gate for your dog on this walk, however this will be inaccessible for very large breeds of dog.

How to get there - From Keswick follow the signs for Borrowdale on the B5289. The road passes close to Derwent Water briefly and then when you reach the water's edge once again, take the next turning on your left, which is signed for Ashness Bridge and parking. Pass the first car park on your left and continue. Just after going over the road bridge turn right into the car park.

Grid Reference - NY 269196   **Nearest Postcode** - CA12 5UR

Parking - Ashness Wood Car Park National Trust Pay and Display

You will need - Dog leads, dog bags

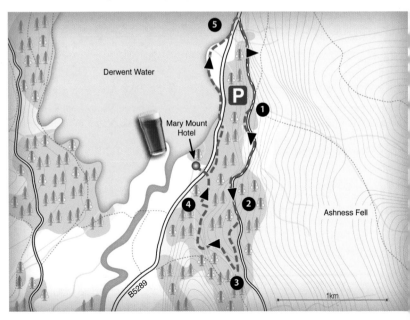

The Walk

❶ Keep your dog under close control or on a lead to begin this walk, as there is a road and there may be sheep grazing freely. From the car park, face the road and take the footpath on the right, near to the ticket dispenser. The path ascends gently to reach the quiet road, on which you continue to ascend. There is mixed broadleaved woodland on both sides of the road.

Continue on the road for some distance. You will pass a house on your right and then pass through a gate to avoid the cattle grid. The scenery is delightful in all directions. If you have your dog off the lead it may be safer to put your dog on a lead before reaching another car park on your left, as there is a cliff edge on your right, where the views are amazing. You can see across Derwent Water to Bassenthwaite Lake and the fells beyond. Continue your ascent on the quiet road. Just as you reach the last lay-by on your left for the car park take a minor path on your right. This path follows close to the road for a while, amongst the woodland. There may be sheep grazing so keep your dog under close control or on a lead. The path is undulating and rocky in places as you step over exposed bedrock. You then pass over a couple of small streams, which may dry up in the summer months. After passing views of Derwent Water the woodland expands on your right.

As you reach close to the road you will meet another wider path. ❷ Turn right on this path and descend into the woodland. Again the path is a little rocky. The woods have lots of larch in this section as well as silver birch and oak trees. Continue to descend and just before reaching the stone wall and gate ahead turn right onto a minor path. ❸ The path switches back and veers to the left, where you will reach close to the river on your left. The path crosses a stream just after you reach the river. Keep to the more defined path to your left, staying with the river. On the opposite side of the river there are rock faces. After passing the rock face look for a minor path which veers to the right slightly. The river is now on your far left and you are walking through the woodland.

Keep the river to your left and continue straight ahead. You will find that the path becomes a little unclear. Persevere for a short distance, as you will soon pick out the path once again. Cross a small stream and then the path becomes visible, as you ascend a little. There are heather pockets and holly in this section of the woodland, which is now dominated by oak.

Ignore a footpath on your right, which ascends, and continue on the level path. The river on your left now veers away. The path descends, and as you reach a sharp bend, take the path on your right. There are views of Derwent Water ahead of you. The path continues to descend through the woodland. On reaching a stile, cross it, using the dog-friendly lift gate. Continue on the well- worn path, which has switchbacks to lessen the gradient. Care should be taken if you have your dog on a lead, as this path can be steep in places, with loose stone making it slippery.

As you reach the second switchback, you can take a short detour left to reach a view point across Derwent Water (recommended in the summer months as leaf cover will have restricted your view). Then come back onto the path to continue your descent. The path will eventually lead you back near to the river. On reaching close to the river, just before the bench ahead and left, take a path on your right (if you go to the bench you can enjoy views of the waterfall Lodore Falls). On reaching a stone wall near to the back of a hotel turn right.

❹ Get ready to put your dog on a lead, as there is a busy road ahead (about 200 yards away) and continue on the well-worn path beside the stone wall.

Ignore a path left, which goes to the road, and continue. You will reach a narrow entrance in the stone wall at the roadside. Cross with care and enter the driveway for The Mary Mount Hotel. Continue, passing the car park on the left where you will reach the glazed entrance. On entering into the hotel porch, don't go through the door on your left, but turn right into the hallway and follow the sign for the bar, where dogs are welcome and you can enjoy a delicious meal and a well-earned rest.

On leaving The Mary Mount cross the road with care and go back into the entrance gap in the stone wall. This time turn left and keep your dog on a lead as the path follows close to the road and there are gaps in the stone wall. Continue on this path for some distance, passing small, moss-covered boulders, beneath the shade of the oak trees.

You will reach another opening in the stone wall, where there is a sign for Kettlewell Car Park. Cross the road here with care. Don't go into the car park, but cross the footbridge and continue on a lakeside path. The stone wall is a little higher here and in good order, but if you wish to let your dog off the lead, keep him under close control as the path follows beside the road for a while. The path veers away from the road and there is farmland on your right, with a stock fence keeping your dog away from the sheep. You can now relax and let your dog enjoy the water's edge. Continue on this path for a little while, where you can enjoy the views as you are surrounded by fells.

Cross a footbridge over a stream and continue close to the stock fence. You are now heading back towards the road, so keep your dog under close control or on a lead. Continue beside the lake, with the road on your right. As you reach a jetty, put your dog on a lead and take the steps on your right, where you will reach the road. ❺ Cross the road with care and ascend on the quiet road ahead, which takes a left turn off the main road. Pass through a gate beside the cattle grid and continue past the car park on your left. There may be sheep grazing freely here. Follow on the road until you cross the road bridge and reach the car park.

8. **Thirlmere** - Kings Head Inn

A former seventeenth century coaching inn situated at the foot of Helvellyn in the heart of The Lake District, The Kings Head is surrounded by spectacular scenery with unsurpassed views toward St Johns in the Vale, Blencathra and Skiddaw. The Kings Head offers a unique dining experience, both offering Traditional English dishes and local specialties created from the finest local produce. In the recently refurbished Bar Restaurant they serve a range of traditional favourites. The bar offers local real ales, fine wines and a range of malt whiskies. The great food and drink here are more than enough reason to drop in during your walk.

The Kings Head has a Lakeland Produce Store offering a wide range of local food, drinks and gifts from the finest Cumbrian producers. The Kings Head also offers dog friendly en suite bedrooms comprising of doubles, twins, single and family rooms, all with views of the surrounding fells.

Tel: 017687 72393

"Eugh, I think I'm gonna feel ruff in the morning!"

Thirlmere - Medium - 2 miles - 1hr 30min
- Challenging - 4.8 miles - 3hrs 30min

This walk starts at the foot of Helvellyn, following a track that can get a little rocky in places. The scenery is wonderful, with views across to Thirlmere and mountainous views ahead as you continue. Mountain streams flow across or under the path in places, allowing your dog to get a cool drink. You will pass a couple of small waterfalls along the way. A stop about a quarter of the way in brings you to The King's Head, where you can enjoy a hearty pub lunch. You then ascend back amongst the crags.

After crossing a road there is a forest with some ascents and then on to Thirlmere Lake. There may be sheep grazing throughout this walk. There is a short section of busy road, which has a path on the grass verge.

How to get there - Follow the A591 from Grasmere to Keswick and look for Swirls car park on the right hand side of the road.

Grid Reference - NY 316168

Parking - Pay and display in Swirls Car Park

You will need - Dog leads, dog bags

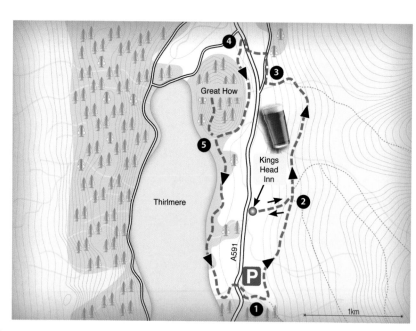

The Walk

❶ Keep your dog on a lead or under close control as there may be sheep grazing. Go to the end of the car park, furthest from the road. Facing the river turn right and head towards the footbridge. Cross the bridge and pass through a small gate. Continue on the well-made path, beside the river.

Stay on the well-made path beside the river, which is signed for Helvellyn. Pass through a gate, cross another footbridge and ascend the path straight ahead. Turn left just before you reach another footbridge and pass through a gate. Now follow the footpath beside the stone wall on your left.

There is a new plantation on your right, with crags above on your far right. On your left you can see Thirlmere. Continue on this path with some exposed rock. The large hill ahead of you is known as Great How. A little further along, pass a narrow path on your left and continue on the main path, which is indicated by a yellow way-marker. The path begins to ascend. Cross a narrow footbridge beside a fabulous waterfall and continue on the path for some distance. Streams cross the path in many areas, where your dog can get refreshment in hot weather. Pass through a gate and continue to the stone wall.

❷ You will reach a finger post at the stone wall. Turn left, following the sign for Thirlspot Farm. Descend on the path, passing through a gate and continue

to descend. Cross the footbridge and continue straight ahead to descend the hillside through farmland. Pass through another gate and descend to the farmyard. Go through the farm gate and cross the farmyard. Pass through another farm gate and cross diagonally to your right to pass through a small gate where you will reach The Kings Head. You can now enjoy a stop at this wonderful pub.

Once refreshed, continue back the way you came for a short section, crossing the farmyard and then ascend the field once again to the gate. Cross the footbridge and turn left to ascend the path beside the stone wall, following the finger post signed for Brown Crag.

On returning to the three-way finger post turn left, following the sign for Stanah and Sticks Pass. Pass through a gate and continue on the path beside the stone wall, ignoring a path that veers to your right. Cross a stream, via stones and continue straight ahead. There are amazing views ahead and on your left. The path gets a little rough over exposed stone in places.

On reaching the corner of the stone wall there is a stunning waterfall on your left. Cross a footbridge ahead and pass through a gate. Continue straight ahead, following the worn rugged path. Ignore a grassy path which crosses the path that you are on, and continue straight ahead.

Pass through another gate and continue beside the stone wall on your left. There are newly-planted trees on your right across the hillside. Streams cross the path in places. Pass through a gate and continue on the path, which turns sharply to follow beside the stone wall. Soon afterwards, the path veers away from the stone wall and descends to a finger post. Continue to another stone wall and pass through the gate on your right (not straight ahead). Follow beside the stone wall, where you will reach another waterfall on your right.

Pass through another gate and follow the worn path, descending towards the large boulder on your left. Pass through a gate and follow the worn grassy path, descending to the stone barn. You can choose to go over the ladder stile to the access track, but if your dog can't cross ladder stiles, continue on the bridleway, turning right, passing beside the stone barn on your left. Put your dog on a lead and pass through the gate and pass beside the back of the farmhouse. Continue to the front of the house on your left and descend on the access road, passing the ladder stile on your left.

❸ Pass garages on your left and houses on your right, and then a recreation hall on your left. On reaching the quiet road, turn right. A little further on look out for a public footpath on your left. On reaching it, pass through the gate and cross the field beside the stone wall on your left.

At the end of the field, ensure your dog is on a lead and pass through the gate, and ascend the steps to the busy main road. Turn right and follow the narrow path on the grass verge. Just before you reach the stone wall on your

right, cross the road and follow the track, signed Lake and Swirls, and Great How. ❹ Although the area is wooded, there may still be sheep grazing.

Continue into Thirlmere Forest with a river below on your left. Continue on the track for some distance, to the edge of the mixed woodland. The path ascends and you will pass a track on your left, which leads to a gate into farmland. The path ascends more steeply for a short section.

On reaching the top of the hill you will have lovely views over Thirlmere. As you descend, just before the bend there is an option of another hill climb as a linear detour to gain amazing views at the top of Great How. ❺ If you wish to go to the top of Great How turn right on the grassy track, which ascends immediately and follow sections A and B. To continue without climbing Great How skip the next paragraphs and follow section B.

Section A.

Take this path to begin your climb, which will rise high above the lake, passing through mature oak woods with glacial boulders. The path will get rocky as you climb higher, following the waymarker and a sign for Great How summit. Once you reach a level grassy path turn right. You may need to ensure that your dog is under close control as there are rock faces with drops on the other side as you approach a bench.

The views here are stunning and you can rest for a while and take it all in. The highest point can be reached just a little further on by taking a left turn, from your sitting position on the bench, on the slightly worn track. You will see a mound of rocks that people have placed. Here you will see panoramic views that are worth all the effort it has taken to get here.

Now it is back down the way that you came. Once you have descended the steeper section and reached the main track, turn right and follow section B.

Secton B.

Continue on the main track, ignoring another path on your right just after, which is indicated by a waymarker. Descend on the main path, beside a stone wall on your left to begin with.

Enjoy the views on your right across the lake, amongst the Scots pines; on your left there are views of the fells in the distance, the highest peak being Helvellyn. After quite a steep descending section the path becomes undulating.

On reaching a stone wall pass through the gateway and take the next narrow path on your right, just after the short descent. Follow this narrow path, with a stone wall on your right. The path will meander, reaching close to the water's edge in places. Cross a couple of small footbridges and pass through a small meadow overlooking the lake. Cross another footbridge, which brings you back into the woods, where beech trees dominate. Pass through a kissing gate and on returning to a main track turn right.

The track cuts through the woodland, with some views of the lake where the trees allow. Again you will come close to the water's edge in places. You will reach a bend to your left, where you leave the lake behind. There is a last ascent following beside a river on your right. You will pass another waterfall and then pass through a gate into a field, where sheep may be grazing. Pass another waterfall and continue on the well-made footpath, where you will reach a gate. Ensure your dog is on a lead, pass through the gate and ascend the steps to a car park, beside the main road. Continue to the right hand side of the edge of the car park and cross the busy road. Pass through a small gate and follow the well-worn path signed for Helvellyn. Ascend the steps and follow the grassy path back to the car park.

9. Knipe Scar - Crown & Mitre

The Crown & Mitre is a 4 star Inn based near Haweswater in Cumbria. Situated in the beautiful hamlet of Bampton Grange, it is an historic free house nestled on the edge of the North Eastern Fells. With a range of fine wines and ales and the highest quality food made from fresh, local ingredients.

What better, than to come in after a bracing day in the hills with your dog to a roaring fire, a pint of real ale (or wine) and some good food. Dogs are also welcome to stay if you fancy a holiday. Whilst situated in a quiet corner of the Lake District National Park, you are never more than a few minutes from the rest of Lakeland, giving you the benefit of easy access to attractions with a quiet haven to come home to.

Tel: 01931 713225
www.crownandmitre.com (check website for opening hours)

hmmm..."no one appreciates the very
special genius of your conversation as I do."

Knipe Scar - Easy - 2.2 miles - 1hr 30min
- Medium - 4.5 miles - 2hrs 30min

There are two choices on this walk, giving you the option of an easy walk or a medium. The medium covers the whole walk, whereas the easy leaves out the ascent to Knipe Scar. The views on reaching Knipe Scar will make it hard to resist, as they are truly breathtaking. You will pass small pockets of limestone pavement on reaching the scar. You then descend to the moorland below, where you will reach a quiet road leading to Knipe Village. Just before reaching the village cross another section of moor, where you will reach a fantastic suspension bridge. Your dog may need some coaxing here, as the bridge is a little scary. Then a peaceful walk along the lovely river will bring you back to Bampton Grange village, where you can enjoy a pub lunch at the Crown and Mitre.

How to get there - Take the Shap turn-off from the M6 (J39). Continue on the B6261 and then the A6, following signs for Shap. Take a left turn from Shap Village, signed for Shap Abbey and Bampton. Continue on this road to reach Bampton Village. The Crown and Mitre will be located on your right hand side. There is parking on the road-side just before it.

Grid Reference - NY 521180   **Postcode** - CA10 2QR
Parking - Free on the road-side at the Crown and Mitre
You will need - Dog leads, dog bags, and water for your dog

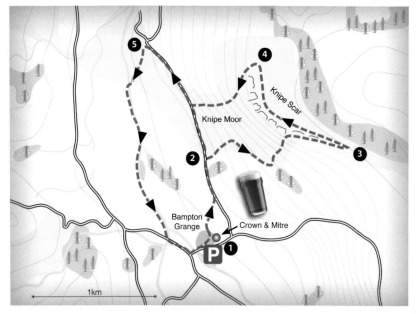

The Walk

❶ Facing the pub go to the left hand side of the pub and pass the gable end on your right. Immediately after passing the pub take the footpath on your right, passing between the houses. On reaching a gate, ensure that your dog is under close control or on a lead and enter the field.

Continue straight ahead across the field and go through the gate at the end of the stone wall. Cross this field diagonally to your left slightly. Head for the corner of the stone wall, near to the large drainage pipe. Cross the stone wall via the squeeze stile and turn left onto a quiet road. On reaching a cattle grid, pass through the gate. There may be sheep grazing so keep your dog under close control or on a lead. **❷** Continue on the road for about 20 yards.

Now if you want to do the easy walk, skip the following paragraphs and continue after the heading Easy Route. If you choose the medium walk continue following the directions below. Take the footpath on your right. Now continue crossing the common, close to the stone wall on your right, ascending slightly, with gorse scrub on your left. The path veers to your left, away from the stone wall as you reach close to the end of the field on your right. On meeting back with the stone wall at the end of the field, turn right. Continue on the grassy path with the bracken bank on your left and the stone wall on your right.

As the path begins to ascend you will then veer to the left, moving away from the stone wall. Take the next path ahead, which is a right turn off the path that

you are on, as you reach a sharp bend. On reaching a gate, don't pass through it but turn left. After about 20 yards you will meet another grassy track. Turn right on the path, which then ascends between the bracken.

The crag ahead is known as Knipe Scar. Ignore a path on your left and continue to ascend towards the crag through an open area of grassland. As you reach gorse and bracken, veer to your right and continue to ascend, heading toward the end of the stone wall on your right. Now follow the well-defined path, with the stone wall on your right. You will have fantastic views on your right and a line of exposed stone on your far left (Knipe Scar). You will reach a disused gate into the field on your right, and then the path will bend to your left and ascend to reach the line of exposed rock.

As you reach the rock the path will become unclear. Veer to your left and continue to ascend the hill. On reaching close to a stone wall ahead you will see a defined, grassy path. ❸ Turn left onto the path and continue. You will now follow on the top of the scar. On your right you will pass small areas of limestone pavement, which is a rare and often protected habitat for specialised plants. On a clear day you can enjoy views in all directions. The grassy path will bend to your right, on meeting with more limestone pavement. You need to leave the path here and veer to your left, where you will be on the edge of the hillside.

Pass the limestone pavement on your right, on a path that is nothing more than a sheep track. You will have amazing views to your left, looking over beautiful countryside for miles with fells in the distance. You can see the paths below, which you have taken on your journey, starting at the village. Keep your dog under close control, as there may be drops over the edge in places. You will reach an Ordinance Survey station at ground level. If there has been

recent rainfall your dog can get a drink as it holds water. Continue on this path for some distance, where you can enjoy the views and the unusual features of the limestone pavement.

Just after passing an obvious, small quarried area on your right, near to the end of the scar, look for a path on your left roughly 100 yards before reaching a stone wall ahead. ❹ Take the path left, which again is nothing more than a sheep track, diagonally to your right across Knipe Moor.

Another track joins your path from your left, and then the path widens and descends between the bracken. As you reach close to a stone wall on your right, the path bends sharply to your left. It then descends into gorse scrub. On reaching level ground, ignore a path that crosses the path you are on and continue straight ahead. Continue amongst the gorse until reaching a quiet road, where you then turn right. You now follow the directions for the easy route.

Easy Route

Continue on the road for some distance. The road cuts through the moor, passing a road on your right. ❺ On reaching a red telephone box, on the edge of Knipe Village, take the footpath on your left, signed for Bampton. Cross the moor, following the narrow, grassy path.

You will reach a beautiful, wide river and then a magnificent suspension bridge. Cross the bridge, giving your dog lots of encouragement, as he may be a little nervous. Turn left and pass through the kissing gate. Now follow beside the river, where if the river is not too swollen, you may let your dog off the lead, as there is a stock fence separating you from any grazing livestock.

The river is tree-lined in places with alder, silver birch and some ash and oak. Pass through a gate and continue, now with wire fence on your right, so keep your dog under close control or on a lead, as he may get into the field. Continue on, and as you get near to a small gate ahead your dog can get close to the river for a drink as the bank peters away. Pass through the gate, into farmland, keeping your dog under close control or on a lead. Stay on the raised path and cross the field. On reaching a stone wall, pass through the gate and cross the field ahead and slightly to your right, heading for the corner of the field.

Pass through the kissing gate onto a road, and turn left. Walk on the right-hand side of the road, with care, as there are no pavements. Continue around the sharp left bend as you reach Bampton Grange Village and cross the road bridge. You will reach the Crown and Mitre pub ahead, where you can have a welcome drink or a good pub lunch.

10. Langdale - Sticklebarn

Sticklebarn is the only National Trust run pub.

Nestled in Langdale's valley bottom you'll find Sticklebarn, with crackling fires, real ales and great food, it's a great place to unwind after a day of walking with your dog.

After your walk you can relax and enjoy a very warm welcome here at the Sticklebarn. They have treats at the ready for you dog and plenty of water dishes supplied.

Tel: 015394 37668
Email: sticklebarn@nationaltrust.org.uk (check website for opening hours)

"Is it ok if I bring a well-behaved human in?"

Stickle Tarn - Challenging - 1.6 miles - 1hr 30min
Langdale Valley - Easy - 2.8 miles - 1hr 30min

If you enjoy rugged scenery, then this walk is for you as it is amongst the fells. You will be following beside Stickle Ghyll all the way, with many streams where your dog can get water and wonderful waterfalls. You will cross stepping-stones over the ghyll to reach Stickle Tarn. On your descent you will be rewarded with the most astounding views, across Langdale Valley. This is a linear walk, therefore you can simply turn around at any point and go back, should the weather turn for the worst. The ascent is continuous, but the gradient is gradual. There are sheep throughout this walk. There are two stiles with dog gates, but for very large breeds of dog the gates will be inaccessible. There is a small section of easy scramble, but if you need to keep your dog on a lead it may prove a little tricky, especially on your descent. Not recommended for old, arthritic dogs.

How to get there - From Ambleside, follow signs for Coniston on the A593. Continue on the B5343 following signs for Great Langdale. About 3-4 miles after passing Chapel Stile. Pass a car park on your left and just after you will reach the National Trust car park on your right.

Grid Reference - NY 294063 **Postcode** – LA22 9JU

Parking - Pay and display, National Trust Car Park

You will need - Dog leads, dog bags

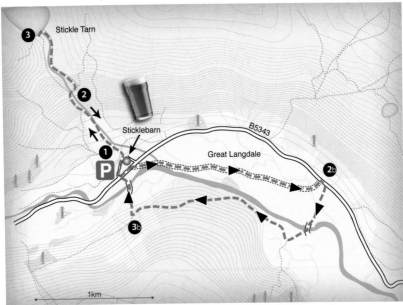

Challenging Walk

❶ From the car park, furthest from the road, head toward the toilet block and the wonderfully crafted shelter, which houses an interpretation panel. Pass the shelter on your right and where you will continue beside the stone wall on your right.

The path passes between a stone wall and a willow screen. Go through the entrance gap in the stone wall and continue straight ahead on the well-worn path. Pass through a gate and ascend the path, ignoring a path on your right.

The path ascends beside the mountain stream on your right, which is called Stickle Ghyll. You will pass through pine trees to begin with. You will reach several small waterfalls along the way, as water pounds over rocks.

There are some stone slab steps after you pass the first waterfall. There are many small streams, which pass over the path, where your dog can get water, without having to go down to the fast flowing stream.

❷ Cross a footbridge over the stream and continue on the path. You will then cross a stile, which has a lift gate for dogs. Continue straight

ahead, crossing another smaller stream. Veer to the right, where you will see the stone path once again, and continue to ascend, beside the stock fence on your right.

You will reach a stock fence ahead, where the path veers away from the stream temporarily, as trees have been screened off from grazing sheep. Cross slate stone slabs over a stream and keep to the right of the exposed rock, where there are steps to ascend.

The path bends to your right, continuing with the stream. As you continue to ascend you will reach some exposed rock. Cross over the rock at the right-hand side, where you will then see the path once again. The path reaches a stream crossing, via the large rock boulders.

After crossing the stream, continue ascending on the path. On reaching another section of exposed stone, you will have an easy scramble. Continue alongside the river, heading for the stone wall, where you will reach Stickle Tarn and the furthest point of your walk.

❸ Now simply turn around and retrace your steps. After crossing the stepping stones and reaching the exposed rock, the easiest path is at the higher point of the rock on your left.

As you descend a little further, you will round a bend, where the views are absolutely brilliant, looking down into the Langdale valley to Little Langdale Tarn and the hills and fells beyond.

Continue your descent, following close to Stickle Ghyll, where you will return to the car park and a warm welcome at the Sticklebarn where you can have a well-earned pub lunch.

Dog Friendly Pub Walks - Lake District

Easy Walk

1 Dogs on leads to begin with. From the National Trust car park go to the furthest end from the entrance and pass the toilet block having it on your left. Walk past the front of the Stickle Barn pub. Go through the pub car park onto the drive and turn right. Once reaching the road cross over and enter the National Park car park. Take the footpath on your left in the far corner.

Once on this path it is safe to let your dog off the lead. The path goes for some distance in the valley between stock fencing with some remnant hedge trees on either side. As you near the end of the track get your dog back on the lead. Once at the end, turn left onto another farm track. **2b** On reaching the road turn right for a short distance. Take the footpath through the kissing gate on the right.

You can let your dogs off the lead here for a short while as you walk between the hedgerows. Note the traditional stone slab field boundaries. Pass through another kissing gate, putting your dogs on leads or under close control and follow the obvious track. Cross a stream/ditch and go through another kissing gate. Go along the middle of the field on the track, where you will path through another kissing gate over a bridge. Follow the farm track ascending towards the farmhouse. Pass the farmhouse on your right. Turn right passing a stone barn. Continue between the stone walls for a while. You are following the Cumbrian Way long distance footpath.

The path goes downhill and through a kissing gate. Stay on this path, which goes uphill again becoming very stony. The views are fantastic of the Langdale Pikes. You will be walking between the hillside and a stone wall. You will pass many glacial boulders along the way following the stone wall on your right. Cross a stone slab bridge over a stream and then enter a stone sheep fold, which is a fine example of traditional craftsmanship.

Go back out of the keep through a gate. It is all downhill from now on. Follow the stone path as you descend the field, heading for the kissing gate. Once through the kissing gate continue straight ahead and pass a gap in the stone wall. You must put your dogs on leads now as you approach the farm house. Walk alongside a stream on your right. Go over the small bridge and through a kissing gate keeping the buildings on your left.

3b Pass through the farm gate and descend the access path crossing through the middle of a field. Go over a bridge to reach the road and then cross with care to the car park.

11. Elterwater - The Britannia Inn

The Britannia Inn is nestled in the breathtaking Langdale Valley at the heart of the English Lake District. The Britannia Inn has scenic views and delicious pub food. There are two individual bar areas for the dog walker and comfortable rooms for those who are on holidays with their dog. There is no charge for your dog when you stay.

After your walk make the most of the pub's open fire and cosy nooks during those long Lake District winter evenings, and spill out into the garden for some stunning alfresco dining under the summer sun. The Britannia Inn really is a pub for all seasons. Pop in for a pint of real ale and a quick lunch, or stay for a few days and enjoy the outstanding Elterwater location. As a Lake District pub offering accommodation, the hospitality is second-to-none. Dogs are welcome in all the bar areas of the pub just not the Dining room or the residents lounge.

Tel: 015394 37210
Email: info@britinn.co.uk
www.thebritanniainn.com (check website for opening hours)

"You've eaten all the meat... and now I've got to beg for the bone?"

Elterwater - Easy - 2.2 miles - 1hr 30min
- Challenging - 4.5 miles - 3hrs 30min

This is truly a stunning walk, following beside The River Brathay, with beautiful scenery across hilly farmland to the rugged fells in the distance. You pass two waterfalls, Skelwith Force and Colwith Force. The walk also passes through lovely oak woodlands, green all year round with mosses and ferns coving the ground, boulders and tree trunks. You will cross some farmland, where sheep may be grazing, and follow small stretches of quiet lanes. There are plenty of streams for your dog to get a drink along the way. There are wooden stiles with dog gates and some stone steps over stone walls on the 'challenging' walk, which will not be suitable for very large breeds of dog.

How to get there - From Ambleside take the A593 to Clappersgate. Follow the signs for Elterwater on the B5343. Once in the village turn left just before the Britannia Inn and park in the National Trust Car Park.

Grid Reference - NY 328048

Nearest Post Code - LA22 9HP

Parking - Pay and display National Trust or free in the Britannia Inn Car Park

You will need - Dog leads, dog bags

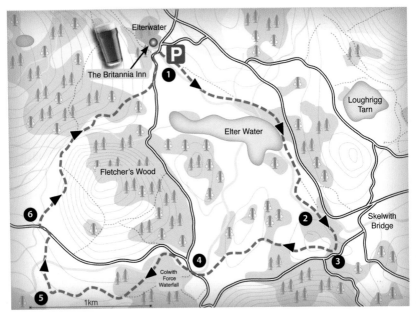

The Walk

❶ From the car park, near to the entrance, face away from the road with the river on your right. Follow beside the stone wall and go through the pedestrian gate. Check the condition of the river, before letting your dog off the lead. After heavy rainfall the fast flow can be dangerous for dogs. Continue on the well-made path beside the stone wall and the river on your right. There are lovely scenes on your left, across hilly fields to the fells beyond.

A little further along, cross a small footbridge and continue on the path. The river is tree-lined, offering shade on hot sunny days. The path soon veers away from the river, and there is woodland carr on your right. Pass a couple of streams as they flow under the path. You will then have mixed woodland on both sides of the path.

Ignore a footpath on your left and continue straight ahead. Pass through a gate, keeping your dog under close control or on a lead, as there may be sheep grazing. There are wonderful views on your right across Elterwater to the Langdales in the distance. This is a popular spot to stop, where your dog can enjoy the water. Continue on the path, amongst the fantastic scenery, surrounded by mountains and wooded crags, amongst the hilly grassland. The river is much slower here as it flows from the lake, but as you continue the river picks up speed, just before you pass through a gate. For those who want to do an easy linear walk, continue past the fabulously-designed bridge, where a little further along you will have stunning views of the waterfall, Skelwith Force. Keep your dog on a lead, as the flow of the river is rapid here. Then simply turn around and retrace your steps back to the car park.

2 For those who want to do the circular walk, cross the bridge and continue on the path, through the mixed woodland. You will have views of the stunning waterfall on your left. Continue on the main footpath with the river over on your left. Pass a house on your left and continue to ascend on the path. Ignore a footpath on your left, signed for Skelwith Bridge and continue straight ahead, following a sign for Colwith Bridge. There is now a stream on your left. Ascend to a kissing gate; keep your dog under close control or on a lead, as there may be sheep grazing. Pass through the kissing gate and continue on the well-made path, crossing the wood pasture, which then opens out to become rugged pastureland. At a junction of paths, turn right. **3** Pass through a farm gate and continue on a path beside a farmhouse.

Pass through a metal kissing gate beside a store. Pass through another kissing gate, now with stunning scenery straight ahead, across hilly, craggy grassland with trees, surrounded by mountains. A stream passes under the path, where your dog can get a cooling drink. Pass through a farm gate and continue on the path with a stock fence on your right and the field on your left. Continue on the path, following the sign for Elterwater/Colwith, ascending between stone walls.

Pass through a farm gate, keeping your dog on a lead, and enter a farmyard. Pass between the farmhouse and store. Continue past a further building on your left and then on your right. On reaching a tarmac path, cross it and follow

the footpath on the opposite side. Cross a stile, using the dog-friendly lift gate and turn left, crossing a stream. Where you reach a stone wall with a stone stile, cross the stile and follow the footpath between the hedges, keeping your dog on a lead or under close control as there are free range hens in the area.

Pass through a gate, ignore the road on your left and continue straight ahead. Pass through the kissing gate on the opposite side of the tarmac path. Continue to descend on the path, keeping dogs on a lead or under close control through the field. Cross another stile, using the lift gate and continue on the edge of a very steep bank.

Descend the steps and cross another stile, with a lift gate. You then continue beside the river on a well-made path. Ensure you have your dog on a lead and cross a stone stile onto a road. ❹ Turn right onto the road and then take the footpath on the left signed for High Park, just before going over the road bridge. Ascend the steps and go through the gate.

Turn right, following the sign for Colwith Force, passing through the mixed broadleaved woodland, which is dominated by oak. Ascend over some exposed rock and follow the well-made path. There is a river below and then the path ascends and veers to your left. On reaching another path turn right. On reaching a stock fence ahead, don't take the path on your left but take a short detour, following the path on your right to view the waterfall. Retrace your steps and then take the path to the left of the stock fence and ascend the steps.

Continue on the path, which passes the waterfall a little higher up. Ignore a path on your right and continue on the well-made fixed stone path, continuing

through the woodland. Pass over a stream, which crosses the path, where your dog can get a drink. Ascend gradually, passing moss-covered boulders that are scattered throughout the woodland. The path then veers to the left, leaving the river behind. Continue to ascend through the trees and on reaching another path and a stone wall turn right and pass through a kissing gate, keeping your dog under close control or on a lead, as there may be sheep grazing.

Turn right, following the blue way-marker keeping to the edge of farmland, beside a stone wall. Pass through another kissing gate and continue on the path, crossing another field. Put your dog on a lead and pass through a kissing gate to enter the driveway of a house, which is on your right. Turn left ascending the driveway to reach a road. Go through the gate to avoid the cattle grid. Turn right and descend the quiet road. Ignore a stile on your right a footpath on your left, and continue on the road toward the house ahead.

There are beautiful views on your right, over farmland to the fells in the distance. **5** Ensuring that your dog is on a lead, pass the house on your right and take a right turn, which is signed Little Langdale to pass on the other side of the house on your right, then cross the drive and go through the gate ahead to descend on a path between the stone walls. At the end of the track put your dog on a lead or under close control; pass through the farm gate and cross the field. Cross over a footbridge and then cross another field on the obvious worn path. Pass a house on your right, put your dog on a lead and pass through the kissing gate onto a quiet road and turn left. **6** Just as you reach a sign for Wilson Place Farm turn right, passing houses on your left. Pass through a small gate and continue straight ahead passing beside a house and stone barn. Leave the farmyard immediately after the stone barn, passing through the gateway and ascend on a stone path to the edge of a field.

Pass through a kissing gate and follow the path between the fields. Pass through another kissing gate and veer left. Cross a small stream and follow the well-worn path across the field. The field is dominated by juncus, a plant that enjoys boggy ground. On reaching the end of the field, pass through the kissing gate onto a wide, well-made path and turn right, following the sign for Elterwater. Descend on this path, with oak dominated woodland on your left and a stone wall on your right. Pass through a farm gate and continue to descend for quite some distance. As a quiet road joins the path from your left, keep your dog under close control or on a lead. You will pass some houses towards the end, where the path becomes tarmac. On reaching another road turn left, and continue with care, as there are no pavements.

Ignore a road on your left and cross the road bridge, where you will pass the car park on your right. Continue on the road, where you will see the Britannia Inn on your left, where you can enjoy a well-earned meal.

Dog Friendly Pub Walks - Lake District

"That was a long walk, but after a pint
I'm starting to feel almost human!"

12. Easedale Tarn - Tweedies Bar

Tweedies Bar is a CAMRA award winning pub and always has a great range of beers on offer with 8 real ale hand pumps and 2 real ciders or perrys on tap. There are beers from all over the UK with local and Scottish breweries being the most prominent.

You and your dog can unwind in front of the log burning fire, relax with a pint of one of the award winning guest ales and satisfy your appetite with a hearty meal. The food at Tweedies Bar is well known throughout the area and widely reputed as the best pub food around. There is a rich and varied menu served both lunchtimes and evenings as well as a frequently changing specials board which features local and seasonal produce prepared in an innovative and tempting style. The Dale Lodge Hotel offers dog friendly accommodation in Grasmere. Dogs are permitted to stay in all bedrooms with the exception of the Mews.

Tel: 015394 35300
www.dalelodgehotel.co.uk (check website for opening hours)

"I find it very worrying when people don't realise that a good ruby wine should never be served chilled"

Easedale Tarn - Medium - 4.5 miles - 2hrs 30min

This walk is truly amazing with stunning scenery and a waterfall named Sourmilk, which seems to grow as you get closer to it. There is a gradual hill for some of the walk, but nothing too steep. The climb is much rewarded on a clear day as the views are breathtaking and once at the top you will be met with Easedale Tarn. It is very atmospheric amongst the hills, and your dog can enjoy the water. This walk is a linear one so you will have the option of turning around at any point, but this is not recommended as the tarn is worth the effort. There are sheep on this walk, with short sections of quiet road. There is water in many areas for your dog to get a drink. You can stop at Tweedies Bar at the end of the walk for a rewarding meal with your dog.

How to get there - Take the A591 for Keswick and follow signs for Grasmere. Turn onto the B5287 and pass the first car park on your right. On reaching the village follow the sign for the car park, turning left.

Grid Reference - NY 336073

Post Code - LA22 9SW

Parking - Pay and display in Broadgate car park

You will need - Dog leads, dog bags

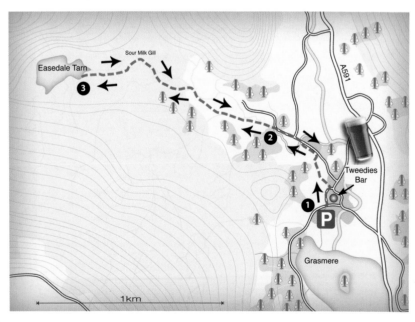

Dog Friendly Pub Walks - Lake District

The Walk

❶ Put your dogs on leads to begin with. From the car park go back onto the road and turn right then immediately left. Pass the hotel and Tweedies Bar on the right and then a row of cottages. Take the first road on the left, passing some houses and head towards the nice gate entrance, taking the gate on the left of the road to avoid the cattle grid.

There may be sheep grazing here. Head back onto the driveway and take the footpath on the right. Follow this path towards the white house. Pass the house and continue straight ahead, and pass through the kissing gate. You may let your dog off the lead here. Walk between the stock fence and the hedgerow, which is beech to begin with.

At the end of this path, put your dog on the lead and go through the gate, and turn left onto the quiet road. Stay on this road until you see a footbridge on the left, which crosses the river.

❷ This is just before you reach Oak Lodge. Once across the footbridge go straight ahead through the trees and over another smaller stone footbridge. Follow this path straight on with a stream on your right. Pass a footbridge on the right and continue straight ahead with a stone wall on your left. Ignore

the footpath to the left. The stone wall will end, to be replaced with a stock fence.

Go through a gate and take the left fork towards Sourmilk Ghyll. Walk straight ahead, through the middle of the field on the stone path. Go through another gate and pass some rocky boulders.

Pass through a kissing gate and then straight on, ascending with a stone wall on your right. Cross a stream as it washes over the rocks via a wooden footbridge. The scenery is stunning in all directions here. Continue uphill where you will soon meet with Sourmilk Ghyll, the stunning waterfall. On each side of the river you will see some juniper amongst the holly, which is native but rare in Britain. As you continue uphill the area flattens out and opens up. You are almost at the furthest point of the walk. A little more uphill and you will reach the tarn following on the worn grassy path.

❸ Once at the tarn it is time for a well-earned rest as you absorb the wonderful atmosphere and scenery. When you are ready, it's back down the way you came. Remember to turn right once you reach the quiet road and look out for the gate on the right. This path runs parallel to the road for a time.

Once through the kissing gate at the end of this path ignore the footpath to the right towards the house and continue on the path meeting with the driveway, turn left, and pass through the gate at the side to avoid the cattle grid. At the end of this road turn right and continue near to the end where you will see Tweedies Bar on your left, where you can enjoy a good pub lunch. On leaving the bar turn left onto the road and you will see the car park at the end of the road.

13. Far Sawrey - Cuckoo Brow Inn

The Cuckoo Brow is situated in the heart of the quiet village of Far Sawrey. It's placed at the top of the hill between Lake Windermere and Hawkshead Village, surrounded by beautiful scenery.

It's a classic, yet contemporary Lake District Bed & Breakfast, which has recently been renovated and restored to its former glory. The manager and staff all love dogs. Water bowls provided in the pub.

They are passionate about the Lakes, and strive to source as much local produce as possible. Ranging from the Real Ales, the game for the Huntsmans Hot Pot or the sausages for the Cumbrian Breakfast, which of course no true Lake District B&B would be without. They also have dog friendly accomodation for those who wish to have a holiday in the Lake District. Food is served all day, 12 noon until 9pm.

Tel: 015394 43425
www.cuckoobrow.co.uk (check website for opening hours)

"Course I'm over 18, check my pawsport!"

Far Sawrey - Medium - 2 miles - 2hrs

This circular walk passes through wonderful woodland, rugged, hilly farmland and beautiful views across countryside and over Windermere. A stop half way along brings you to the delightful Cuckoo Brow Inn, where you can stop for a good rest and lunch. There are many streams, where your dog can get a drink, and you will pass a Victorian folly, known as Claife Viewing Station. There are some ascents on this walk, but nothing too steep, and a short section of quiet road. Sheep may be grazing in parts of this walk. Some paths can get water-logged and a little rugged over exposed stone. There is a section of steep descent, which can be tricky if your dog needs to stay on a lead.

How to get there - Take the B5285 from Hawkshead to Far Sawrey. Once at Far Sawrey follow the signs to Windermere via the ferry. When you reach the lakeside look out for the car park on the left, before the road goes over the bridge to the ferry.

Grid Reference - SD 388954   **Nearest Post Code -** LA22 0LP

Parking - National Trust Ash Landing Car Park Pay and Display

You will need - Dog leads, dog bags

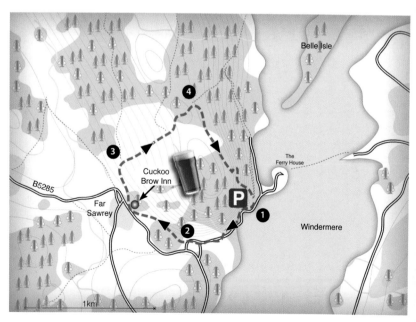

The Walk

1 Keep your dog on a lead to begin this walk. From the car park face the road and turn right, taking the footpath signed Near Sawrey and Hill Top. The path follows alongside the road and there are no boundary fences. You can see Lake Windermere on your left and there are mixed woodlands on your right. On reaching a gate, pass through it and cross the road. Go through a gate on your right (not the one straight ahead) and follow the sign on the finger post for Near Sawrey and Hill Top. Continue along the well-made footpath, with farmland on your left and the road on your right.

On reaching a gate straight ahead pass through it and ascend the steps to the road. Continue to ascend on the road, with care. **2** Take a footpath on the right hand side of the road, just before reaching the second bend, again signed for Near Sawrey Hill Top. Pass between the stone gateposts and ascend on the track amongst the trees and rhododendron. There is a stock fence on your left and estate fencing on your right, followed by a stone wall on your left, cloaked in mosses and ferns.

Cross an access track to a house and then pass through the kissing gate, keeping your dog on a lead or under close control as there may be sheep grazing. Pass a house on your left following beside a stone wall on your left, walking across the edge of a hilly field with exposed rock.

On reaching the corner of the field, pass through a gate, keeping your dog on a lead or under close control as there are houses ahead and a road. Follow on the path, alongside a stone wall on your right, passing another house. You will reach an access road and continue, passing a driveway to a house on your right. Stay on the access track, passing a field on your left. At the bend continue straight ahead, passing a green on your left and a house on your right. Pass a couple of driveways and then pass through a kissing gate and descend the stone track until you reach the road. Turn right on the road and descend to the Cuckoo Brow Inn, where you can take light refreshments or stop for a good pub lunch.

To continue your walk on leaving the pub turn left onto the road and just after passing the pub car park take the bridleway on your left, signed for Belle Grange. You will now be rising to the back of the Cuckoo Brow. Pass The Sawrey Institute on your right and just after you will pass a stream that collects into an old water trough on your right, where your dog can get a drink. Continue on the path, which ascends between two stock fences. There are stunning views on your left, across the hilly countryside.

Continue between the stone walls and then pass through a gate, keeping your dog on a lead or under close control as there may be sheep grazing. Continue on the track with the stone wall on your left, walking on the edge of a hilly field with hawthorn on your right. Ignore a track that veers to your left, as you leave the stone wall and continue on the main track. There are more extensive, stunning views on your left. The path meets back with the stone wall on your left, and you are surrounded by hilly, rugged fields, with wooded rocky crags. Continue on, beside the stone wall.

❸ At the end of the stone wall pass through a farm gate, which is straight ahead of you and continue straight ahead, following the way marker for

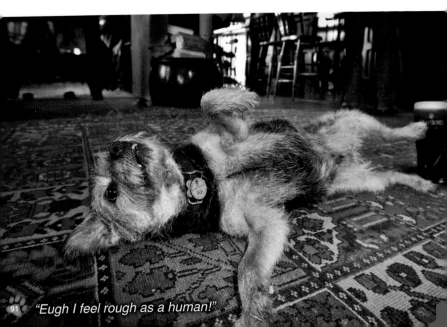

"Eugh I feel rough as a human!"

Windermere Lake Shore and Ferry. Follow beside the stone wall on your left and the stock fence on your right. Keep dogs under close control or on a lead, as the stone wall is dilapidated in places and there may be sheep grazing. Continue on the track, passing through a gate straight ahead of you and then stay on the track between the stone walls. Look out for a small pedestrian gate on your right, signed for Ferry. ❹ Pass through the gate and descend between the stone wall and the stock fence, through mixed woodland. Be careful with your dog as there may be sheep grazing the area.

On reaching the end of the stone wall on your left continue straight ahead on the well-worn path, following the stock fence on your right. Cross a small stream, where your dog can get water. You will now have a stone wall on your left once again. Continue on the path, which will soon veer away from the stock fence. There are views on your left of Lake Windermere through gaps in the trees. The path can get a little rugged as you ascend over the exposed stone. You will reach a stock fence on your left for a short distance.

Take a path on your left, following the sign for Ferry, leaving the stock fence once again. Keep left and descend a steep wooded hillside with switchbacks, heading towards the lake in the distance. The path is quite steep in places so take extra care if you have your dog on a lead. There are some steps along this path in places as you continue through the woodland.

Ferns dominate the woodland floor, with ferns and mosses growing on the bark of the trees, and there are lots of exposed rocks covered with moss. You will pass closely between exposed rocks and then you will reach a Victorian folly, known as Claife Viewing Station. Just after passing the folly descend the steps on your right, following the sign for Ash Landing. At the bottom of the steps, keep your dog under close control and turn right and follow the well-worn path back to the car park.

Breath of Fresh Ale! Hawkshead Wainwright

14. Scout Scar - The Wheatsheaf Inn

The Wheatsheaf has been delightfully refurbished with a real "feel" of a Cumbrian Inn. The pub has a series of rooms and cosy corners, log fires, comfy chairs, and a very inviting bar area serving an excellent selection of local ales and brews.

A treats jar (as pictured to the right) is always ready for your dog to be truly spoilt. The managers and staff are all dog lovers and you will feel more than comfortable bringing your dog here.

Great dining is offered to suit all tastes; old favourites, and a few more; handmade pizzas, Cumbrian delicacies, including, of course, the all important Cumberland sausage! Wherever you sit, you'll enjoy a very warm welcome, and a hearty plateful!

Tel: 015395 68938
www.thewheatsheafbrigsteer.co.uk (check website for opening hours)

Toby's new job as bar manager went down a treat. Especially with the new tips jar in place.

94

Scout Scar - Medium - 3.6 miles - 2hrs 30min

This is a beautiful walk, beginning in Underbarrow, where you will have wonderful views from Scout Scar across beautiful countryside to the sea. There are cliff edges at this point. You will descend into woodland, then cross farmland, where there may be sheep grazing. A forest walk then brings you to Brigsteer Village, where you can rest at the delightful Wheatsheaf Pub. There may be cattle and sheep grazing on this walk. The cattle are of a gentle breed. There is a stone stile on the second part of the walk and an ascent, but nothing too steep, just enough to walk off your lunch.

How to get there - From the A6 in Kendal follow the sign for Underbarrow and Brigsteer. Continue following the sign for Underbarrow and Crosthwaite. Before reaching the village pass the first car park on your right and look for the next car park on the right hand side of the road. If you are following a sat-nav you will stop before reaching the first car park, therefore you will need to continue on a little further.

Grid Reference - SD 489924   **Nearest Postcode** - LA8 8HA

Parking - Free in the car park

You will need - Dog leads, dog bags

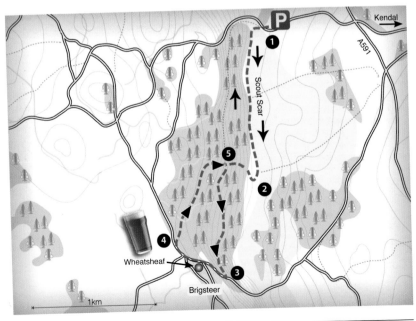

The Walk

❶ Keep your dog on a lead to begin this walk. From the car park head towards the road, but take the footpath on your right before reaching it. On reaching the end of the path cross the road and pass through the kissing gate.

Ascend on a well-made path, but keep your dog under close control or on a lead, as there is a cliff edge ahead and there may be sheep and cattle grazing. Continue on the path between the trees and scrub. You will gain views on your right of the surrounding countryside.

As you reach the sharp bend to your left you will have reached the cliff edge, known as Scout Scar. The views extend for miles here and are quite breathtaking. Continue along the cliff face a little further. You will see a four-way shelter ahead, known as 'The Mushroom'. On reaching 'The Mushroom' you will have views in all directions on a clear day.

Continue on the path, passing 'The Mushroom' on your right, and with the cliff face on your far right. You will pass amongst young ash trees and scrub. Always be aware that there may also be rabbits: if

96

your dog is not under close control or on a lead, he may chase them and run toward the cliff edge.

Continue on this path for some time, following close to Scout Scar. You will have sea views ahead as you continue. On reaching a stone wall pass through the opening. Continue on the main path, amongst some scatterings of heather and juniper.

A little further along the path joins with another wider path. Continue straight ahead, towards the cairn (rock pile). Ignore the path on your left and continue straight ahead, passing the cairn on your left and then immediately veer to your right. ❷ You are now descending.

On reaching the fork (about 20 yards on), take the narrow path on your right. Continue to descend on the worn path, which has a switchback as you descend into a woodland copse. The path can get a little rocky as you descend over the exposed stone. On reaching the edge of the woodland, keep your dog on a lead or under close control and pass through the farm gate into agricultural land. Continue straight ahead. The path joins a farm track, which descends to Barrowfield Farm. Continue straight ahead at the end of the stone wall and head towards the stone barn.

Pass through a gate, which passes the gable end of the barn (not the gate into the yard). Follow between the stone wall and the stock fence and continue on the track, which bends to your left. Follow the pointer on the finger post, signed Brigsteer Road. Go through the small gate to avoid the cattle grid.

Turn right almost immediately, marked by a finger post into the woods. Continue on the well-worn path through the woodland. In autumn after leaf fall, the path may be a little unclear, but there are waymarkers along the route. Continue through the mixed woodland, with farmland on your left and Scout Scar on your far left in the distance. You will meet briefly with a stone wall on your left.

The path descends and then ascends to meet the access road, where you turn right. Continue on this track through the woods, listening out for any farm/forestry vehicles, following beside a stone wall on your left. On reaching the end of the stone wall, the woods clear on your left.

Continue on the track and when you pass a bench on your right you will need to get your dog on a lead, as there is a road ahead. You then pass beside a cattle grid and on reaching the road ❸ turn right and descend into the village, where you will see The Wheatsheaf ahead. Please enter the pub from the car park, where you will find a boot and paw wash if you need it. You can now have a well-earned rest and relax in this wonderful pub.

On leaving the pub, pass through the car park and turn left onto the road and descend, taking care, as there are no pavements. Pass the houses on your left and the village hall on your right. Pass two roads on your left, one signed for Lyth Valley. Just as you leave Brigsteer village you will see a car park on your right a little further along the road.

❹ Go into the car park and at the far end pass into the forest, ascending on the forest track. As the path levels out there are some mixed broadleaved trees amongst the coniferous trees. A stream passes under the path on your left, just before another ascent, where your dog can get a drink.

The path ascends now for about 400 yards. As the path levels off again there are oak and silver birch trees, with bracken-dominated clearings. On your right you can see Scout Scar in the distance. You will pass a small pond on your right, which you may not notice, but which your dog will seek out if he needs to cool down. The path ascends again for a short distance. Just as you reach a yellow warning sign for overhead electric power lines, turn right, ascending on a narrow footpath, indicated by a way-marker. The path backtracks to begin with. There are pockets of heather, but the area is mostly dominated by bracken, with natural regenerating oak, silver birch and holly.

The path may be encroached in the summer months, when the bracken dominates in places. As you reach a stone wall there is a stone stile. Keep your dog under close control or on a lead, as there may be sheep grazing. Cross the stile, which has a greater drop on the other side. Cross the field, heading for the kissing gate on the other side, veering slightly to your left.

Pass through the kissing gate and continue straight ahead on the stony path through the woods. Put your dog on a lead and pass through another kissing gate. Head up the hill, towards the farmhouse. You will see a finger post, just before you reach the house.

5 Turn right on the farm track and then left, following the sign for Scout Scar. You are now on a familiar path. Pass between the stone walls straight ahead, and then follow beside the stock fence on your right, until reaching the farm gate straight ahead (not the farm gate on the left or the farm gate into the field). Pass through the farm gate and continue on the track, with the stone wall on your left and the stock fence on your right. Scout Scar is directly ahead. The path veers away from the wall as you ascend. On reaching a stone wall, pass through a gate into woodland. Take the familiar footpath, which ascends through the woods.

Remember, as you get to the top you will be near to the cliff edge once again and there may be sheep and cattle in the area, so keep your dog under close control or on a lead. After leaving the shade of the trees look out for a path on your left, just as the gradient lessens. Take this path, which switches back as it heads toward the cliff face. Well before reaching the cliff face you will see a fork in the path. Take the inside path on your right. You will then see the cairn, passing it on your right. Continue straight ahead, ignoring a path on your right. After about 100 yards, take the path which veers to your right, continuing to retrace your steps on this path, which will lead back to the familiar four-way shelter.

After passing the four-way shelter, you may wish to continue straight ahead on an inner path to avoid the cliff face, keeping your dog under close control, and pass through the scrub. You will reach the wider path, where you will turn right. Follow the well-made path back to the kissing gate. Put your dog on a lead, pass through the kissing gate and cross the road and follow the path back to the car park.

15. Grizedale - Eagles Head

This 400 year old country pub set in the heart of the Grizedale forest welcomes you with a wood burning stove, low beamed ceilings, dog treats on the bar and water bowls for everyone. This family run business is owned by Simon and Emma selling local cask ales, often from Hawkshead, Barngates and Loweswater breweries. A selection of fine wines compliment the kitchen, which offers home cooked traditional food.

Simon's individual pies are very popular and the Venison burgers are a great twist on the classic. The kitchen also offers daily specials, authentic curries and homemade deserts. There is a large beer garden for those sunny days and warm evenings.

Tel: 01229860237
www.eagleshead.co.uk (check website for opening hours)
email: theeagleshead@gmail.com

"Don't worry, you guys go to the bar
....and I'll look after the pie!"

Grizedale Forest - Medium - 3.4 miles - 2hrs 30min

This circular walk is packed with adventure. Starting with beautiful scenic views across the valley as you ascend gradually through mixed broadleaved woodland. The path then takes you through a forest plantation. You will join briefly onto a cycle track, where you will pass a tranquil tarn and then back into mixed broadleaved woodland. You will pass some delightful short waterfalls as you descend through the woods, following the river. There are some great wooden sculptures to look out for along the way. A steep ascent through beautiful woodland with moss-covered boulders brings you back into the forest. There is a small section of farmland to cross and a small section of quiet road. Your dog will find plenty of water along the way. Some of the paths are a little rough in places. There are a couple of stiles, which have generously sized dog gates.

How to get there - From Hawkshead follow the signs for Grizedale Forest on the B5285. Continue on this road, passing several Forestry Commission car parks. Pass through Satterthwaite Village, where you will pass The Eagle's Head on your right and continue out of the village for about a quarter of a mile, where you will see the small car park on your right.

Grid Reference - NY 349 065   **Post Code** - LA12 8LN

Parking - Pay and Display

You will need - Dog leads, dog bags

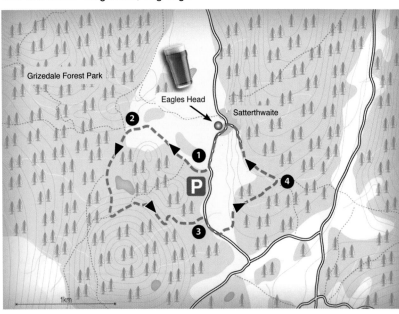

The Walk

❶ From the car park take the bridleway signed Moor Lane and ascend beside a stone wall and farmland on your right, with mixed broadleaved woodland on your left. Ignore a path soon after on your left, and continue ascending to the edge of woodland.

Ignore a footpath on your left. As you ascend you will gain views on your right across the valley, over lovely hilly farmland with rocky outcrops and mature oak and ash trees. Continue on the bridleway, and further along you will be between stone walls. You will pass an old water trough on your left, just after passing a farm gate into a field. You will reach a gate straight ahead, go through the gate and take the footpath immediately on your left. Follow beside the stone wall on your left, with mixed broadleaved woodland on your right. The path soon enters into the forest. You will reach a wider forest track. ❷ Turn left on the forest track and ignore the track immediately on your left.

This track can be popular with cyclists, therefore keep your dog under close control or on a lead, especially during weekends and holiday periods. Continue on this path, ignoring a footpath on your right. You will pass a tarn on your left. A little further along look out for a waymarker on your right, but don't turn right, turn left, leaving the main track and follow the worn narrow path through the forest.

On reaching a wider path turn left and descend. Soon you will reach a main

forest track. Turn right and continue to descend. A stream flows on your left, where you will see small waterfalls in places. Ignore a track on your right and continue where you round a sharp bend. Now you enter into mixed broadleaved woodland.

Continue to descend, crossing the stream as it flows under the path. Stay on the wide track, where the stream is now on your right. You will pass another waterfall, with a lovely water feature, carved from the trees taken from the woodland. Ignore a path on your left and descend to the gate. Cross the stile, using the dog gate provided. Keep your dog under close control or on a lead, as there may be livestock grazing. You are now in wood pasture. Continue on the track, where you will reach another stile just before reaching the road.

❸ Put your dog on a lead, cross the stile and turn right onto the road. Pass a house on your right and then a picnic bench and river on your left. Cross the road bridge and turn immediately left onto an access path, keeping your dog under close control. Pass fields on your left and then a house on your right. Ignore a path on your right and continue. You will now have mixed broadleaved woodland on both sides of the path.

Take the next footpath on your right, which is signed for Bowkerstead Walk. The path ascends amongst the woodland, quite steeply in places. The path can get rough, with larger loose stone. Follow the white marker posts, staying on the worn path. After passing a large wooden sculpture, which is a bench with shelter where you can have a rest after your climb, go through the gap in the stone wall and continue on the worn path.

You will reach a wider track, where you are now on level ground and at the highest point of your walk. There are moss-covered boulders, and ferns on the forest floor, with silver birch amongst the coniferous trees. ❹ On reaching a waymarker for a public bridleway on your right, don't turn right, but turn left. Descend on the path, crossing over some exposed stone in places.

Pass between old wooden gateposts where you will see a stream passing under the path. Continue to descend with a stone wall on your left and farmland beyond. There are mixed broadleaved woodland, dominated by oaks on your right. On reaching a level section the path is well made once again. You can see Satterthwaite Village on your left. Just after another short descent put your dog on a lead as you will soon pass houses and an access road to the village. Turn right on reaching the lane and continue beside the stone wall and farmland on your left. Pass several houses as you reach the edge of the village.

Pass the church on your right and turn left onto the road. You will soon reach The Eagle's Head on your right, where you can get a well-earned pub lunch. On leaving the pub turn right onto the road and continue, leaving the village, where you will soon reach the car park on your right.

Wet Nose Publishing team
- hard at it with the research!

Homemade **Dog Treats**
Recipe Book

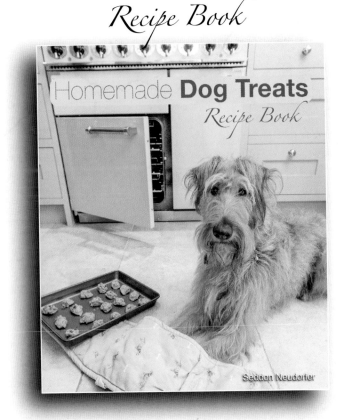

100% Natural

The Homemade Dog Treats Recipe book provides entertainment and inspiration for dog lovers that want to give their dogs healthy and nutritious treats.

Beautifully designed, it is packed with full colour photography and easy to follow recipes. Ingredient that can be found in any supermarket. This book will appeal to anyone who loves dogs or anyone who wants to buy the perfect present. Available now on our web site!

www.countrysidedogwalks.co.uk